Charles H. Parkhurst

**Our Fight with Tammany**

Charles H. Parkhurst

**Our Fight with Tammany**

ISBN/EAN: 9783337373023

Printed in Europe, USA, Canada, Australia, Japan

Cover: Foto ©ninafisch / pixelio.de

More available books at **www.hansebooks.com**

# OUR FIGHT WITH TAMMANY

BY

REV. CHARLES H. PARKHURST, D.D.

NEW YORK
CHARLES SCRIBNER'S SONS
1895

# CONTENTS

### CHAPTER I.
PAGE
THE SOCIETY FOR THE PREVENTION OF CRIME, . . 1

### CHAPTER II.
THE MADISON SQUARE PULPIT'S ANALYSIS OF TAMMANY, 8

### CHAPTER III.
DISCOURSE OF FEBRUARY 14, REVIEWED AND REVILED, . 26

### CHAPTER IV.
REBUKED BY THE GRAND JURY, 38

### CHAPTER V.
COLLECTING EVIDENCE, . . 49

### CHAPTER VI.
AFFIDAVITS IN THE PULPIT, . 59

### CHAPTER VII.
PRESENTMENT BY THE GRAND JURY AGAINST THE POLICE DEPARTMENT, . 70

## CHAPTER VIII.
Byrnes and the "Great Shake-up," . . . 88

## CHAPTER IX.
On the Rack, . . . . . . . 101

## CHAPTER X.
Mass Meeting at Cooper Union, . . . 113

## CHAPTER XI.
The Pulpit and Politics, . . . 128

## CHAPTER XII.
Gardner's Arrest and Trial, . . . 142

## CHAPTER XIII.
The Social Evil, . . . . . 154

## CHAPTER XIV.
Byrnes's Effort to Discredit the Crusade, . 165

## CHAPTER XV.
First Attack on Devery, . . . . 177

## CHAPTER XVI.
Denunciation and Whitewash, . . . 189

## CONTENTS

### CHAPTER XVII.
The Broome Street Mob, . 202

### CHAPTER XVIII.
War on the Captains, . 214

### CHAPTER XIX.
The Chamber of Commerce Appeals to Albany, . 231

### CHAPTER XX.
The Senatorial Investigating Committee, . 240

### CHAPTER XXI.
The Committee of Seventy, . . 253

### CHAPTER XXII.
Election Appeal from the Madison Square Pulpit, . 267

### CHAPTER XXIII.
Victory — Its Perils and Opportunities, . 285

# OUR FIGHT WITH TAMMANY

## CHAPTER I

### THE SOCIETY FOR THE PREVENTION OF CRIME

THE purpose in these pages is to set forth, as briefly and connectedly as possible, the steps that conducted to the overthrow of Tammany Hall on November 6, 1894. The writer does not claim to have handled the matter exhaustively, and has limited himself quite closely to those features in the case upon which he can speak with the authority of an actor or a witness.

We have been doubly motived to this recital. In the first place, although there seems to have been a good deal of desultory warfare waged during the past three years, we are concerned to have our fellow-citizens appreciate the thread of identity of purpose upon which all apparent desultoriness has been strung. We should like, also, to be of service to other municipalities in our country which may still be suffering the same kind of tyranny which our own city has just renounced. Frequent appeals are reaching us from those who would like to have reproduced elsewhere the results which have been secured here, and who seek from us such assistance as we may be able to render. It has seemed that we can in no way so well accede to such requests as by exhibiting, in as simple a manner as possible, the general outline of events in our own town. This is not to deny that each city has its own special and distinguishing conditions. At the same time, as regards the main point at issue, all American cities of any considerable size are substantially circumstanced in much the same way. Virtue is at the bottom and knavery on top. The rascals are out of jail and standing guard over men who aim to be honorable and law-abiding. Statesmanship has very largely degenerated into small and dirty politics. Cities are administered in the pocket interests of the municipal government, not in the moral, social, industrial, and economic behest of the rank and file of the citizens. Something has been done in New York in the way of reversing this policy. If it can be done here it can be done in any city in the Union; and it is not in any spirit of arrogance or conceit that we say that perhaps other cities, still in the condition in which we have been, may be able to learn something from the way in which we have succeeded in escaping from that condition.

However numerous and effective the influences which in these last months have been operating to the overthrow of Tammany, the primary movement in that direction, it is conceded, dates from the reorganization and activity of the Society for the Prevention of Crime. This Society was organized in October, 1878, and the names of the incorporators are as follows:

Peter Cooper,
Howard Crosby,
William H. Wickham,
Benjamin Tatham,
William F. Mott,
Erastus D. Culver,
William B. Merritt,
S. Irenæus Prime,
David J. Whitney,
Frederick A. Booth,
Oscar E. Schmidt,
D. B. St. John Roosa,
Henry Drisler,
Alonzo Follett,
William P. Prentice,
Geo. G. Wheelock,
John H. Hinton.

The original incorporators organized in the election of Dr. Howard Crosby as President, which position he continued to hold until his death, which occurred March 29, 1891; and to such degree was its policy shaped by his wisdom and animated by his spirit that it was publicly known as "Dr. Crosby's Society."

It was through Dr. Crosby's personal influence that I (if I may be permitted to speak of myself in the first person singular) became associated with the Society for the Prevention of Crime. On the morning of Sunday, October 26, 1890, a little more than a week, therefore, prior to the annual election of that year, I preached in the pulpit of the Madison Square Church a sermon bearing upon election issues, which was printed the next morning in one of the daily journals and arrested Dr. Crosby's attention.

The next day he addressed me the following letter, which is here reproduced in *fac-simile*, which is richly characteristic of the good Doctor, both in matter and chirography :

My membership in the Society dates from November 6, 1890, and between that time and the death of Dr. Crosby, the Society held but six meetings—quite insufficient to familiarize a novitiate with the Society's *personnel* and methods. My election as President of the Society occurred on April 30, 1891. My acceptance of such position I made conditional upon the Society's adoption of a policy which has since obtained in all of its operations, and which has been so determinative of all that has transpired later as to require distinct notice at this point.

Somewhat prior to the date of my first connection with the Society I had become knowing to a condition of things throughout the city, of which, during all the years of my residence in town up to that date, I had been ignorant, and of which, except for a special cause, I should probably have continued ignorant. My interest in the congregation to which I minister, made up as it is quite largely of young men, induced in me a special concern for young men and for the conditions under which their urban life has to maintain itself. Through acquaintance with them, and in consequence of information which I gathered from trusted members both of the legal and medical pro-

115 E. 19. Oct. 28/90

My dear Dr. Parkhurst

Will you consent to become one of our Board of Directors of the Soc.y for the Prevention of Crime? I know you are crowded with duties. Alas! So are we all. But we must preserve this city — & our Society has done a great deal in this direction. Kittredge & myself are the only pastors ~~Chapman~~ in the work. Your countenance would be a great help. We meet once a month, and the money raising is in the hands of a financial Committee & does not burden the Clergymen members.

\* \* \* \* \*

Yours ever truly

Howard Busby

fessions, I became easily familiar with certain facts which make out a large feature in the life of the city ; and it occurred to me whether there might not be some means by which, in association with others, I could operate to reduce the strain of current temptation and make it at least a little easier for a city young man to maintain himself at his best.

After the above matter had gone through due process of fermentation in my own mind, I commenced to push out quietly in the two directions of the gambling evil and the social evil, and the first obstruction against which I ran was the Police ! The Department which, in my rustic innocence, I had supposed existed for the purpose of repressing crime, it now began to dawn upon me, had for its principal object to protect and foster crime and make capital out of it. It was a rude awakening to a cruel fact, but it was a fact in the light of which the last three years have been constantly lived.

It was that appreciation of the situation, as thus awakened, that I insisted, upon my election to the Presidency of the Society for the Prevention of Crime, should henceforth determine the Society's policy. Previously the Society had worked in conjunction with the Police. I made it conditional upon my acceptance of the Presidency that the Society should henceforth deal with the Police as its arch-antagonist, making with it no alliance and giving it no quarter. We are the only organization of a similar character in the town that does not consent to lean on the arm of the Police Department; and, in view of the thoroughly rotten character which that Department has been demonstrated to possess, our peculiarity in that particular is one of which we think we have reason to be proud. Repeated efforts have been made by the Police, or by their friends, to draw us into relations of compromise and co-operation. The temptation has, in one or two instances, been strong to yield to such overtures, and doubtless, had the step been taken, there would have been a large and gratifying issue of immediate results; but it would have been at the surrender of our vantage-ground, and what we should have gained in superficial victory we should have sacrificed in substantial power.

That, then, was one feature of the policy adopted by the Society at its reorganization in 1891; we determined to fight the disease and not the symptoms. The second feature followed on naturally from that. Hitherto the Society, through its Executive Committee and its agents, had contented itself with dealing with small infractions of the law, such as arresting bartenders for selling to minors; raiding saloons and disorderly houses that had not sufficient "pull" to render impossible the serving of a warrant. From that time on the Society commenced to gun for large game.

The late David J. Whitney, one of the original corporate members of the Society, with a heart as tender as that of a child, but a very Samson in all the qualities of a born fighter, advocated this modification of policy with characteristic energy and enthusiasm, and there is no living member of the Society but wishes that our ardent and beloved old colleague might have survived to witness the overthrow of the rascals whom he hated with so intelligent and relentless a hatred. Such, then, were the elements of policy, in pursuance of which the reorganized Society in 1891 commenced its work—" Down with the Police" and " No Shot for Diminutive Game."

# CHAPTER II

### THE MADISON SQUARE PULPIT'S ANALYSIS OF TAMMANY

THE events related in the previous chapter led up to the discharge of what may perhaps be called, "The First Gun of the Campaign," the sermon preached in Madison Square Church, Sabbath morning, February 14, 1892.

No notice had been given of its delivery and no one was less suspicious than the preacher himself of the disturbing effect it would produce. He was so thoroughly persuaded of the truth he spoke, that it came to him as a surprise that community should become in any degree wrought up over it. As one of the links in the chain of sequence, the discourse is here inserted substantially as delivered.

"*Ye are the salt of the earth.*"—Matthew v. 13.

That states illustratively the entire situation. It characterizes the world we live in; it defines the functions of the Christianity that has entered into the world, and it indicates by implication the stint which it devolves upon each Christian man and woman of us to help to perform. These words of our text occur in what we have learned to know as "The Sermon on the Mount," or what we might properly designate as Christ's statement of fundamentals. In this sermon He is putting in His preliminary work: He is laying a basis broad and deep enough to carry everything that will be laid upon it later. And it is one of the impressive features of the matter that the Founder of Christianity so distinctly foresaw that practical and concrete relation with the world into which the new faith was to come, and that so early in His ministry as this He announced that relation in terms so simple and unmistakable.

Ye are the salt of the earth. This, then, is a corrupt world, and Christianity is the antiseptic that is to be rubbed into it in order to arrest the process of its decay. An illustration taken from common things, but which states at a stroke the entire story. The reason for selecting the above Scripture, and the burden that is upon my mind this morning is this: that current Christianity seems not in any notable or conspicuous way to be fulfilling the destiny which the Lord here appoints for it. It lacks distinct purpose, and it lacks virility. We are living in a wicked world, and we are fallen upon bad times. And the question that has been pressing upon my heart these days and weeks past has been—What can I do?

We are not thinking just now so much of the world at large as we are of the particular part of the world that it is our painful privilege to live in. We are not saying that the times are any worse than they have been ; but the evil that is in them is giving most uncommonly distinct tokens of its presence and vitality, and it is making a good many earnest people serious. They are asking, What is to be done ? What is there that I can do ? In its municipal life our city is thoroughly rotten. Here is an immense city reaching out arms of evangelization to every quarter of the globe ; and yet every step that we take looking to the moral betterment of this city has to be taken directly in the teeth of the damnable pack of administrative bloodhounds that are fattening themselves on the ethical flesh and blood of our citizenship.

We have a right to demand that the Mayor and those associated with him in administering the affairs of this municipality should not put obstructions in the path of our ameliorating endeavors ; and they do. There is not a form under which the devil disguises himself that so perplexes us in our efforts, or so bewilders us in the devising of our schemes as the polluted harpies that, under the pretence of governing this city, are feeding day and night on its quivering vitals. They are a lying, perjured, rum-soaked, and libidinous lot. If we try to close up a house of prostitution or of assignation, we, in the guilelessness of our innocent imaginations, might have supposed that the arm of the city government that takes official cognizance of such matters, would like nothing so well as to watch daytimes and sit up nights for the purpose of bringing these dirty malefactors to their deserts. On the contrary, the arm of the city government that takes official cognizance of such matters evinces but a languid interest, shows no genius in ferreting out crime, prosecutes only when it has to, and has a mind so keenly judicial that almost no amount of evidence that can be heaped up is accepted as sufficient to warrant indictment.

We do not say that the proposition to raid any noted house of assignation touches our city government at a sensitive spot. We do not say that they frequent them; nor do we say that it is money in their pockets to have them maintained. We only say (we think a good deal more, but we only say) that so far as relates to the blotting out of such houses the strength of the municipal administration is practically leagued with them rather than arrayed against them.

The same holds true of other institutions of an allied character. Gambling-houses flourish on all these streets almost as thick as roses in Sharon. They are open to the initiated at any hour of day or night. They are eating into the character of some of what we are accustomed to think of as our best and most promising young men. They are a sly and constant menace to all that is choicest and most vigorous in a moral way in the generation that is now moving on to the field of action. If we try to close up a gambling-house, we, in the guilelessness of our innocent imaginations, might have supposed that the arm of the city government that takes cognizance of such matters would find no service so congenial as that of combining with well-intentioned citizens in turning up the light on these nefarious dens and giving to the public certified lists of the names of their frequenters. But if you convict a man of keeping a gambling hell in this town you have got to do it in spite of the authorities and not by the aid of the authorities.

It was only this past week that a search-warrant was issued by one of the courts in town, and before the officer with his posse reached No. 522 Sixth Avenue, the action of the court reached there, and the house that is spoken of in Scripture as empty, swept, and garnished, was not, in point of unadorned vacuity, a circumstance to the innocent barrenness of the gambling-rooms in question. I do not say that the judge of Jefferson Market Police Court was responsible for the slip. I do not believe that he was, at least in any direct way. All that is intended by the reference is that the police court leaked. With hardly the shadow of a doubt that court, in some one of its subordinates at any rate, stands in with the gamblers, and to that degree the court becomes the criminal's protector and guardian angel. This is mentioned only as illustration of the fact that some people understand, and that all people ought to understand, that crime in this city is intrenched in our municipal administration, and that what ought to be a bulwark against crime is a stronghold in its defence. We strike the same difficulty again when we come to matters of excise.

No one can have followed the crusade that has been in progress these last weeks against unlicensed saloons or against saloons that have been open in unlicensed hours, and have a solitary shred of doubt that every conviction of a saloon-keeper is obtainable only by a square fight with the constituted authorities. The police do not take the initiative. What has been done during the last six weeks has been done because the outraged sentiment of decent people voicing itself through the press has rendered it impossible for what we amuse ourselves by calling the guardians of the public peace and virtue, vulgarly known as the police, to do otherwise than bring some criminals to justice, or at least to threaten to do so. Unless all signs are misleading, your average policeman or your average police captain is not going to disturb a criminal, if the criminal has means, if he can help it.

We are saying nothing as to the connection there is between the criminal's means and the policeman's indulgence. We only state in explanation that it is the universal opinion of those who have studied longest and most deeply into the municipal criminality of this city, that every crime here has its price. I am not saying that that is so, but that the more intently any man of brains scrutinizes these matters the more he discovers along this line that is of an intensely interesting nature. I should not be surprised to know that every building in this town in which gambling or prostitution or the illicit sale of liquor is carried on has immunity secured to it by a scale of police taxation that is as carefully graded and as thoroughly systematized as any that obtains in the assessment of personal property or real estate that is made for the purpose of meeting municipal, State, or Federal expenses current. The facts do not always get to the surface, but when they do they let in a great lot of light into the subterranean mysteries of this rum-besotted and Tammany-debauched town.

Near the beginning of the year the Grand Jury considered the matter of indicting the keeper of a notorious resort on Fourteenth Street. (I am giving the case as it was presented in one of our most trustworthy journals, and has, I believe, not been contradicted). There was no legal evidence at hand that would be sufficient to convict, and the District-Attorney was asked to secure some. An innocent imagination would have supposed that he would jump at the opportunity. The request was repeated by the Grand Jury, apparently without effect. His hesitancy may have been due to either one of two causes. He may have known so much about the establishment that he did not like to touch it, or he may have known so little about it that he was sceptical as to the truth of the derogatory reports that were in circulation in regard to it. Indeed, the District-Attorney said to me in his own house four weeks ago that until after McGlory's establishment was raided he had no idea that institutions of so vile a character existed in this city. All we can say is that we must give the young man the benefit of the doubt. Such a case is truly affecting. Innocence like that in so wicked a town ought not to be allowed to go abroad after dark without an escort. But to return to our narrative.

Our guileless District-Attorney, with the down of unsuspecting innocence upon his blushing cheek, failed to respond to the demands for evidence made upon him by the Grand Jury. The jurors themselves, therefore, assumed experimentally the character of detectives, and the proprietor of the place was soon caught, of course, in the act of illegal selling. An indictment was then found. It remained to secure witnesses that would be willing to go on the stand and testify; for while the jurors were willing to visit the place and satisfy their own minds of the illegality of what was going on there, they experienced a natural delicacy in having their names publicly associated with such a resort in the published reports of criminal procedure. Accordingly instructions were given to the captain of the precinct to procure the necessary evidence. This was followed by another touching exhibition of modesty and blushing hesitancy. The fact of it is they all stand in with each other. It is simply one solid gang of rascals, half of the gang in office and the other half out, and the two halves steadily catering to each other across the official line. The captain declared reiteratedly that evidence against McGlory was something that he could not obtain, till finally the Grand Jury threatened to indict the captain himself, whereupon the evidence was at once produced and McGlory convicted upon it. All of which is only another way of saying that the most effective allies which McGlory had in the prosecution of his vile trade on Fourteenth Street were the District-Attorney and the captain of the precinct.

Now it may be said that this method of stating the case is injudicious; that it is unwise too sharply to antagonize the powers that be; that convictions will not be obtainable if we make enemies of the men who exercise police and judicial functions. On the contrary, there are only two kinds of argument that exercise the slightest logical urgency on the minds of that stripe of bandit—one is money and the other is fear. We shall gain nothing by disguising the facts. To call things by their right names is always a direct contribution to wholesome effects. A steamer can only make half-time in a fog. The first necessity of battle is to have the combatants clearly and easily distinguishable by the diversity of their uniform. We want to know what is what.

Every solid statement of fact is argument. Every time you deal with things as they are, and name them in honest, ringing Saxon, you have done something. It has always been trump-card in the devil's game to keep things mixed. He mixed them in Paradise, and he has been trying to keep them mixed ever since. If the powers that are managing this town are supremely and concertedly bent on encouraging iniquity in order to the strengthening of their own position, and the enlargement of their own capital, what, in Heaven's name, is the use of disguising the fact and wrapping it up in ambiguous euphemisms ?

Something like a year ago, in company with a number of gentlemen, I conferred in his office with the highest municipal dignitary of this city in regard to the slovenly and the wicked way in which he was pretending to clean our streets. In what I had to say to him at that time I addressed him as though he were a man, and as though he had the supreme interests of this city at heart ; and I have been ashamed of myself from the crown of my head to the sole of my foot ever since. Saying nothing about the outrage a man commits upon himself by the conscious falsification of facts, it does not pay. Neither the devil nor any of his minions can be caught in a trap. You can hammer him, but you cannot snare him. Cajolery only lubricates the machinery of his iniquity. Petting him oils the bearings; minimizes the squeak and maximizes the velocity. Now this is not spoken in malice. It is not spoken without a recognition of the fact that there are men occupying official place in this city whose chief ambition it is to discharge their duties incorruptibly. Of course such exceptions are due to circumstances that it was beyond the power of dominant influence to control. We have referred to such exceptions only for the purpose of anticipating the charge that our indictment has been harsh and indiscriminate.

But after all that has been said the great fact remains untouched and uninvalidated, that every effort that is made to improve character in this city, every effort to make men respectable, honest, temperate, and sexually clean is a direct blow between the eyes of the Mayor and his whole gang of drunken and lecherous subordinates, in this sense that while we fight iniquity they shield and patronize it; while we try to convert criminals they manufacture them; and they have a hundred dollars invested in manufacturing machinery to our one invested in converting machinery. And there is no scheme in this direction too colossal for their ambition to plan and to push. At this very time, in reliance upon the energies of evil that dominate this city, there is being urged at Albany the passage of a bill that will have for its effect to leave the number of liquor licenses unrestricted, to forbid all attempts to obtain proof of illicit sales, to legalize the sale of liquor after one o'clock on Sunday afternoon, and indeed to keep open bar 160 out of 168 hours of every week. Sin never gets tired; never is low-spirited; has the courage of its convictions; never fritters away its power and its genius pettifogging over side issues. What voluminous lessons the saints might learn from the sinners!

We speak of these things because it is our business as the pastor of a Christian church to speak of them. You know that we are not slow to insist upon keenness of spiritual discernment, or upon the reticent vigor of a life hid with Christ in God. Piety is the genius of the entire matter ; but piety, when it fronts sin, has got to become grit. Salt is a concrete commodity, and requires to be rubbed into the very pores of decay. I scarcely ever move into the midst of the busier parts of this town without feeling in a pained way how little of actual touch there is between the life of the church and the life of the times. As we saw last Sabbath morning, we must have a consciousness of God, but the truth complementary to that is that we must have just as lively a consciousness of the world we are living in. Men ought to have that, and women ought to have it too. Nobody that can read is excusable for not knowing what is transpiring. And Christians of either sex ought to know it and ought to want to know it ; ought to feel that it is part of their own legitimate concern to know it.

We have no criticism to pass on the effort to improve the quality of the civilization in Central Africa, but it would count more in the moral life of the world to have this city, where the heart of the country beats, dominated in its life and government by the ethical principles insisted on by the Gospel, than to have a belt of evangelical light a hundred miles broad thrown clear across the Dark Continent. And the men and women that live here are the ones to do it. It is achievable. What Christianity has done Christianity can do. And when it is done it is going to be done by the men and women who stand up and make a business of the thing, and quit playing with it; quit imagining that somehow we are going, by some indescribable means, to drift into a better state of things.

Say all you please about the might of the Holy Ghost, every step in the history of an ameliorated civilization has cost just so much personal push. You and I have something to do about it. If we have a brain, or a heart, or a purse, and sit still and let things take their course, making no sign, uttering no protest, flinging ourselves into no endeavor, the times will eventually sit in judgment upon us, and they will damn us. Christianity is here for an object. The salt is here for a purpose. If your Christianity is not vigorous enough to help save this country and this city, it is not vigorous enough to do anything toward saving you. Reality is not worn out. The truth is not knock-kneed. The incisive edge of bare-bladed righteousness will still cut. Only it has got to be righteousness that is not afraid to stand up, move into the midst of iniquity and shake itself. The humanly incarnated principles of this Gospel were able in three centuries to change the moral complexion of the whole Roman Empire; and there is nothing the matter with the Christianity here except that the incarnations of it are lazy and cowardly, and think more of their personal comfort than they do of municipal decency, and more of their dollars than they do of a city that is governed by men who are not tricky and beastly.

But you ask me perhaps what is the use of all this asseveration and vituperation; what is the good of protesting? What is the good of protesting? Do you know what the word Protestant means? Do you know that a Protestant is nothing but a protestant? A man who protests? And did not the men who protested in the sixteenth century do a good deal? Didn't they start a volcano beneath the crust of the whole of European civilization? Wherever you have a Luther, a grand stick of human timber, all afire with holy indignation, a man of God, who is not too lymphatic to get off his knees, or too cowardly to come out of his closet, confront iniquity, look it in the eye, plaster it with its baptismal name—such a man can start a reformation and a revolution every day in the year if there are enough of them to go around. Why, it makes no difference how thick the darkness is, a ray of light will cut it if it is healthy and spry.

Do you know that the newspapers had not been solidly at work for more than about four weeks before the dives began to close up? Why, the truth will frighten even a policeman, if you will lodge it where David did when he fired at Goliath. Truth, with explosive enough behind it, would scare even the captain of a precinct, and chase the blushes from the callow face of the District-Attorney. We have had an example of that recently on a larger scale in the matter of the Louisiana lottery. The whole country was kindled into a flame of indignation, and the lottery men bowed before the storm. And, so far as the North was concerned, it was principally the doing of one man, too, a man who had a head, heart, and convictions, and a pen and lungs to back them.

You see that these things do not go by arithmetic, nor by a show of hands. A man who is held in the grip of the everlasting truth and is not afraid is a young army in himself. That is exactly what the Bible means when it says that one man shall chase a thousand. That is the way history has always gone. That is what the Bible story of Sodom means and the assurance that ten men would have sufficed to save it. Not ten that were scared, but ten men that so had the courage of their convictions, and that so appreciated the priestliness of the office to which they had been called that the multitudinousness of the dirty crowd they stood up among neither dashed their confidence nor quenched their testimony.

This is not bringing politics into the pulpit, politics as such. The particular political stripe of a municipal administration is no matter of our interest, and none of our business; but to strike at iniquity is a part of the business of the Church; indeed, it is the business of the Church. It is primarily what the Church is for, no matter in what connection that sin may find itself associated and intermixed. If it fall properly within the jurisdiction of this church to try to convert Third Avenue drunkards from their alcoholism, then certainly it is germane to the functions of this church to strike the sturdiest blows it is capable of at a municipal administration whose supreme mission it is to protect, foster, and propagate alcoholism. If it is proper for us to go around cleaning up after the devil, it is proper for us to fight the devil. If it is right to cure, it is right to prevent, and a thousand times more economical and sagacious. If we are not, as a church, transcending our jurisdiction by attempting to convert Third Avenue prostitutes from their harlotry, then surely we are within the pale of our authority as a church when we antagonize and bear prophetic testimony against an administration the one necessary outcome of whose policy it is to breed prostitutes. Republicans and Democrats we have nothing to do with, but sin it is our particular province to ferret out, to publish, and in unadorned Saxon to stigmatize; and the more influential the position in which that sin is intrenched, the more painstaking and pronounced requires to be our analysis, and the more exempt from hesitancy and euphemism our characterization.

The only object of my appeal this morning has been to sound a distinct note, and to quicken our Christian sense of the obligatory relation in which we stand toward the official and administrative criminality that is filthifying our entire municipal life, making New York a very hot-bed of knavery, debauchery, and bestiality, in the atmosphere of which, and at the corrosive touch of which, there is not a young man so noble, nor a young girl so pure, as not to be in a degree infected by the fetid contamination. There is no malice in this, any more than there would be if we were talking about cannibalism in the South Sea Islands; only that having to live in the midst of it, and having to pay taxes to help support it, and having nine-tenths of our Christian effort neutralized and paralyzed by the damnable pressure of it, naturally our thoughts are strained to a little snugger tension.

I have meant to be unprejudiced in my position, and conservative in my demands, but, Christian friends, we have got to have a better world, and we have got to have a better city than this is, and men who feel iniquity keenly and who are not afraid to stand up and hammer it unflinchingly and remorselessly, and never get tired of hammering it, are the instruments God has always used to the defeat of Satan and to the bringing in of a better day. The good Lord take the fog out of our eyes, the paralysis out of our nerves, and the limp out of our muscles, and the meanness out of our praise, show to us our duty, and reveal to us our superb opportunity, making of every man and woman among us a prophet, instinct with a longing so intense that we shall not be afraid, loving righteousness with a loyalty so impassioned that we shall feel the might of it and trust it, and our lives become this day enlisted in the maintenance of the right, and thus show that Almighty God is mightier than all the ranks of Satan that challenge His claims and dispute His blessed progress.

# CHAPTER III.

### DISCOURSE OF FEBRUARY 14, REVIEWED AND REVILED.

THE discourse recorded in the foregoing chapter was largely reproduced in the daily journals appearing the next morning. The editorial comments which it provoked helped to show the general attitude of the public mind at the time, and the reader will probably be pleased to have a number of them quoted at this point as an essential part of the narrative. Most of these extracts criticised the discourse adversely; but, as in almost every case the journals from which quotations are made have since that time become vigorous and unflinching in their warfare against the same evils and evil-doers against which the discourse itself was directed, we have in no instance specified the authorship of the extracts. This book is not written for the purpose of paying off old scores, but with the design of giving an honest history of the campaign.

"The ability of the Rev. Dr. Parkhurst, pastor of the Madison Square Presbyterian Church of New York, in the use of vituperative epithet, unsparing denunciation, and intemperate anathema, has been for some time fully recognized. His public utterances, which have most attracted attention, have been of the malediction type, whether applied to theological wrestling with his associate divines, or used in cursings of municipal authorities. His latest objects of attack are the city officers of New York, whom he lashes and characterizes as a 'damnable pack of administrative bloodhounds.' An uneducated person, covering in public the scope of the condemnation effort of Dr. Parkhurst last Sunday, would probably, by our laws, get 'ten dollars, or thirty days in the workhouse' at the hands of Judge Cowing."

"Rev. Dr. Parkhurst, of New York, fired a broadside at the Tammany tiger last Sunday that has raised howls from all parts of the Democratic jungle, and a dozen cubs are snapping and snarling at the good man's heels. There is little cause for hope that the ugly brute can yet be driven from his lair, but it will do no harm to give him an occasional stirring up from the pulpit or through the press."

"Dr. Parkhurst undertook to say too much—and said it. His is just the kind of opposition or denunciation on which public offenders thrive. A mentor or a muzzle is what he needs. He mistakes epithets for epigrams."

"Yesterday he delivered probably the most scathing denunciation of the present administrative government of New York, which means Tammany Hall, ever uttered, not excepting political speeches during a campaign. Some portions of this striking address are reproduced in our columns to-day. They should be considered in connection with Hon. Richard Croker's article in the current *North American Review*. Croker is Grand Sachem of Tammany Hall, and in the article referred to, he not only defends Tammany control of New York, but claims that it ought to be extended, and brazenly declares war to the knife on any citizens who, in their love of good government, dare to oppose Tammany, openly or in secret."

"Dr. Parkhurst's sermon on the iniquity of Tammany will serve to strengthen the impression that the less the pulpit has to do with politics the better, even though it be vice that is struck at. The whole responsibility for setting the world right does not rest with the clergy. The newspapers are capable of doing a good deal of preaching themselves, and Dr. Parkhurst perhaps has invaded their field."

"The Rev. Dr. Parkhurst's vigorous arraignment of our local administration has aroused the wrath of those whom he charged with promoting vice and crime and corruption in this city. There is no reason to regret the manifestation of distress by anybody whom the preacher's shafts pierced, but if that is the only effect produced the gain will be small. Denunciation of the rulers of New York was not the end of Dr. Parkhurst's discourse. He designed it rather to be the means of arousing his hearers and as many other citizens as possible to a sense of their own responsibility for the fact and consequences of bad government. Such utterances are useful because they at least tend to create and stimulate public sentiment, and their ultimate value cannot be exactly measured by the immediate effects which they produce. But it is a shame and a pity that they are so largely wasted. For it must be acknowledged that the visible results of vigorous and repeated assaults upon the secret society by which New York is pillaged and variously maltreated are not conspicuous.

"Dr. Parkhurst has done as much as one man can do by a single appeal to arouse the community from this moral lethargy. What will his sermon accomplish? Something, we hope, yet we fear very little. But those who heard, or have read it, if they are in sympathy with its purpose, cannot escape the responsibility imposed on them. They can make it potent, if they will."

"The habit of some emotional preachers of reflecting upon the characters and habits of public officials, or people who do not subscribe to their ultra views on social questions, got the Rev. Dr. Parkhurst, of the Madison Square Presbyterian Church in New York, in trouble. The officials of New York City are talking about calling upon him to substantiate his charge that they are a lying, rum-soaked, libidinous lot, before the Grand Jury. If he fails to do this, then they contemplate having him indicted as a slanderer.

"Men in the pulpit have no more right to slander their fellow-men than anybody else. They are, in fact, under a greater moral obligation than other men to refrain from making accusations or repeating statements that they cannot verify under oath. The pulpit would have more influence in the affairs of life if all preachers were controlled in their criticisms of public men and measures by a strict observance of this obligation."

"It is believed that Dr. Parkhurst's remarks to-morrow will be less scathing and virulent than those of a week previous. The doctor has been engaged during the past few days in picking the bird shot of public opinion out of his anatomy, and is in a somewhat subdued and chastened spirit, we take it."

"The Rev. Charles H. Parkhurst has given New Yorkers something to think about. His sermon yesterday was directed against the evils of the city government with extreme vigor. Indeed so fierce were the speaker's denunciations, so wholesale his charges, and so reckless his insinuations, that it may be questioned whether the sermon will produce much effect upon thinking men. New York is not well governed, but probably the city knows it as well as Mr. Parkhurst."

"We hope that every good citizen of New York will read the admirable report of the Rev. Dr. Charles H. Parkhurst's rousing sermon yesterday morning at the Madison Square Presbyterian Church.

"It was the severest indictment of this Tammany-debauched municipal government that has been made. It is a good sign when the ministers of this city find time and tongue to denounce our monstrous misgovernment. More than one eloquent preacher has of late raised his voice in protest against the iniquities with which we are surrounded and the oppression under which we live.

"The slumbering indignation of the people is beginning to break forth like a volcano, and its echoes will not die out until the rascals have been turned out."

"The Rev. Dr. Parkhurst 'took on dreadful' last Sunday. With well feigned virtuous indignation he rhetorically assaulted the whole municipal outfit, plainly stating that the officials, from Mayor Grant down to the latest Dago appointment in Tom Brennan's street-cleaning force, were the silent partners of all the enterprising criminals in town.

"Dr. Parkhurst would be entitled to all the way from five to five hundred years' penal servitude for such an assertion, if it were to be levelled at specific individuals. The city government of New York may not be free from corruption, but the bulk of our officials are gentlemen of character and honesty.

"Dr. Parkhurst is not a safe guide.

"If he knows no more of Christianity than he does of politics he will be likely to lead his flock of sheep into a moral quagmire, and, perhaps, to a certain frequently mentioned bottomless pit.

"The reverend doctor should have remembered the commandment, 'Thou shalt not bear false witness against thy neighbor,' an offence not far removed from murder, since it may kill a reputation and ruin a life.

"Invective to be effective should be pointed with the shining arrow of truth."

"Tammany Hall still keeps up its pretence of being inexpressibly shocked at the 'sad degradation' of the pulpit by Dr. Parkhurst of the Madison Square Presbyterian Church. It would suit Tammany exactly if the pulpit were to keep its artillery trained on the wickedness of man before the flood, or try to reduce and capture the Tower of Babel, or to blow daylight through the persecuting Emperor Nero. Indeed Tammany does not care if it comes down to as modern a theme as the sceptical chestnuts of the eighteenth century.

"But when it begins on nineteenth century crime, corruption, and public robbery, Tammany's delicate moral sense, Tammany's exquisite religious tact, Tammany's fervor for the gospel of mediæval theology is aroused, and the Rev. Dr. Parkhurst is unanimously pronounced—by Tammany—a shameless debaser and abuser of the pulpit."

"These are specific charges. If they are true, the public officers concerned ought to be impeached and imprisoned as the abettors of crime, the partners of criminals, false servants of the people, and characters dangerous to the community and disgraceful to civilization. As they are specific charges, it is, of course, incumbent on this preacher to sustain them with specific facts and proofs.

"He made them publicly, and uttered them within a house of Divine worship, as if they were the words of God Himself. He denounced the officers of the municipal government as a whole, and these officers in particular, as utterly vile and rotten, the fosterers of crime instead of its prosecutors. Either he spoke from knowledge and with precise facts to support his infamous charges, or he is a vile liar and slanderer, who should be driven from the Christian pulpit and subjected by the civil law to the criminal punishment he deserves.

"Let Dr. Parkhurst, therefore, be called upon to substantiate his charges before the Grand Jury, so that the men he denounces thus specifically may be indicted, tried, and punished ; or if he is unable to present any facts justifying them, let him be indicted, tried, and punished himself as a wicked, malicious, reckless, and criminal slanderer.

" District-Attorney Nicoll owes it to the preacher, to himself, and to the interests of justice generally, to bring to account the Rev. Charles H. Parkhurst, D. D. His charges as uttered from the Madison Square pulpit have been published to all the world, and as coming from such a source they will be believed very widely and cause great damage to the reputation of the individuals assailed and of the community which keeps them in office. Hence it is the imperative duty of the District-Attorney to take proceedings to make Dr. Parkhurst prove his words or be made criminally answerable for them."

" A general denunciation like that of Dr. Parkhurst creates indignation in the breasts of such officials, and leads to reprisals, which generate sympathy. In this way reaction is brought about, which negatives the good aimed at by the preacher. *It is also an injury to religion, because it lowers the public estimate of the judgment which issues from the pulpit.* We are far from thinking that a clergyman should not denounce wickedness in high or low places, whether the parties be in official or private station, but such denunciations should be calm and dispassionate, and, above all, they should be free from exaggeration ; for, unless this be the case, they do more harm than good."

" It is not at all likely that such sermons as that preached by Dr. Parkhurst in Madison Square Presbyterian Church, Sunday morning last, make the world any better; and it is certain that such violent and intemperate utterances from the pulpit do the Church positive injury.

"It is not news that Tammany is worldly and wicked, but it is not becoming in a minister of the gospel to loudly proclaim from the pulpit that 'they are a lying, perjured, rum-soaked, and lascivious lot.'"

"The Rev. Charles H. Parkhurst ought to read and ponder that one of the commandments which condemns the bearing of false witness, and that passage which has something to say about 'railing accusations.' He will do well to reflect upon the impropriety of extravagant overstatement, the sin of exaggeration, and the care a clergyman should take to know what he is talking about before indulging in the intemperate abuse and denunciation of his fellow-men. There is much to criticise in New York municipal government, but nothing to excuse so violent an outburst of vituperation as that which Mr. Parkhurst preached for a sermon yesterday. A delicate regard for truth and justice is as important in the pulpit as elsewhere."

"One Parkhurst, who bears by courtesy and custom the title 'reverend,' and preaches the gospel according to St. Billingsgate from the pulpit of the Madison Square Presbyterian Church, New York, attacked all the officials of that city last Sunday, calling them collectively 'a damnable pack of administrative bloodhounds,' 'polluted harpies,' and 'a lying, perjured, rum-soaked, and libidinous lot." Furthermore, the reverend gentleman, standing under the consecrated

roof of the holy edifice, declared that 'every effort to
make men respectable, honest, temperate, and sexually
clean is a direct blow between the eyes of the Mayor
and his whole gang of drunken and lecherous subordinates.' There was a time when reckless vituperation and 'slangwhanging' of this sort disgraced the
editorial columns of the press and afforded satirists
theme for stinging caricatures."

To these editorial criticisms I will only add three or
four extracts from reported interviews with as many
city officials.

Police Captain —— said

" That it was a shame for a minister of the Gospel
to disgrace the pulpit by such utterances.

" When he says that the heads of the departments
in this city are a lying, drunken class he deliberately
tells a falsehood. No man of good judgment would
utter such a thing about men who are so temperate,
reliable, and honorable."

"Such intemperate utterances," said Public Works
Commissioner ——

"Answer themselves. They have no weight with
sensible people. It is doubtless true that the municipal government is open to criticism, as everything
human must be. It is even possible that abuses exist
in some of the departments ; but if we are to have reforms they can never be brought about by such palpable misstatements of facts. This minister of the
Gospel shows a most uncharitable spirit in his intem-

perate ravings, and violates the first law of Christianity, by stating what he knows to be false, if he knows anything about it."

Another public official indicated his jealous concern for the cause of Christianity in these terms:

"Dr. Parkhurst violates the command which says, 'Thou shalt not bear false witness against thy neighbor.' His discourse was unworthy of the man and of the place. It is just such utterances that belittle the influence of the clergy and retard the cause of Christianity."

It is a singular, but by no means inexplicable coincidence, that those officials that are most in league with crime, and those journals that are most distinctly representative of the gambling-table and the brothel, were the ones that in their criticisms most profusely affected the phrases of piety and wept the bitterest tears over the dishonor I had put upon the pulpit and the Christian ministry.

Commissioner —— of the Police Board said:

"Ordinarily, language of this kind should be passed over without notice, but the harsh tone of Mr. Parkhurst's sermon is unchristianlike, and if allowed to go unnoticed would be a tacit admission of guilt.

"Heretofore, I believe, Dr. Parkhurst has been devoting himself to preaching the Gospel and doing good, but when he stoops to such abuse of public officials, and that from the pulpit, he ought to lose caste among his own listeners.

"The language used by the gentleman is vulgar. It is a libel upon the city when he says that every crime has its price. If such a thing as protection by the police does exist, it is his duty to come forward with the information.

"I should not be surprised, however, if this is not the beginning of a series of tirades finding its nucleus in a new political movement intended to antagonize and combat a certain political organization. I will, however, be charitable, and admit that Dr. Parkhurst has been imposed upon by some people who have come to him with stories of the alleged deplorable condition of our city."

Police Commissioner —— said :

"Everything the doctor said was untrue. It would seem as if it were meant as a political movement in opposition to Tammany."

If there was any doubt in his mind then, as to what it "meant," he is probably well over his uncertainty now.

## CHAPTER IV

### REBUKED BY THE GRAND JURY

IN my discourse of February 14th, I had said nothing that was not true, but I had said a good many things that I was not at that time in a condition to prove. The air was full of feathers and fur, indicating that a variety of flying fowl and creeping beast had been hit; but I had waked up a whole jungle of teeth-gnashing brutes, and it was a question whether the hunter was going to bag the game or the game make prey of the hunter.

The demand was openly made that I should either prove my charges or be prosecuted for libel. Legal talent, as eminent as any the town afforded, was immediately put at my gratuitous service in case libel suits should be pressed. It soon began to be rumored that the District-Attorney was planning to experiment on me before the Grand Jury. Of course the City Hall authorities appreciated the truth of the charges I had made, and that was just what was the matter; and if they had supposed that I could substantiate my charges, the thing they would most studiously and affectionately have done would have been to let me alone. But they were of the opinion (and the fact justified the opinion) that I had not fortified myself with the details of legal proof necessary to substantiate my charges, and they were willing to take the risk of applying the mild inquisition of the Grand Jury, knowing that the secrecy under which that tribunal conducts its séances would help to secure suspected officials from inconvenience in case it should turn out that I knew more than they supposed. It is impossible not to remark, parenthetically, what a convenient arrangement a Grand Jury may prove to be, if its members can be "trusted," and there is a problematic field of inquiry which the District-Attorney's office would like to have traversed without involving itself or its friends in any considerable peril.

Naturally enough, a subpœna was issued requiring my attendance before the Grand Jury. This was on the 23d of February. It was not as difficult to get before the Grand Jury then as it has been a good many times since. The atmosphere of the room was distinctly uncongenial. I was not able to inform the Jury that the charges which I had made had their foundation in anything other than uncontradicted newspaper statements. Whether they said that it was an indictable offence for me to accuse officials of criminality with which reputable journals systematically charged them without being indicted, I do not remember,—that is, I am not at liberty to repeat. The sum and substance of it all was that I could not swear as of my own knowledge that the District-Attorney had lived an immoral life, that police officers were blackmailers, that police justices encouraged bunco-steering and abortion, or that the entire Tammany organization was not a disguised wing of the Prohibition Party; and the foreman politely indicated to me that further attendance on my part would not be required.

As I recall that session it occurs to me to say that while I did not give them a great deal, I learned a lot. I was distinctly worsted; cheerful, but whipped. As I withdrew from that august presence I recorded in my heart a solemn vow, five years long, that I would never again be caught in the presence of the enemy without powder and shot in my gun-barrel. It was severe schooling, but I shall be wiser clear into the next world for what I learned on the 23d of February.

One week later, on the first day of March, the Grand Jury issued its presentment, which, while not mentioning the name of the offender, was evidently enough designed as a rebuke for the terms in which I had referred to the District-Attorney in particular, and to the members of the municipal administration in general.

The text of the presentment was as follows:

*To the Court of General Sessions of the Peace of the City and County of New York:*
*To the Hon. Randolph B. Martine, Presiding Judge:*

During the present term of this court there were published in the journals of this city, as the accounts of a discourse delivered from the pulpit of one of our churches, certain accusations against the characters and fitness of the officials charged with the duty of administering our municipal government.

The imputations were not limited to any particular branch of the city government, but in sweeping terms condemned the entire body of officials in language so lacking in specification, however, that, with one exception, no cognizance could be taken of them.

One assertion, however, was sufficiently specific as to warrant attention by this body, namely, the declaration to the effect that the District-Attorney had, in November, 1891, refused to supply, although in his power to do so, evidence required by the Grand Jury then in session, for the purpose of founding a prosecution against a notorious and disreputable resort, the proprietor of which has since been convicted and is now undergoing the penalty of the law; and that by such refusal and neglecting to proceed against the proprietor of such resort, the District-Attorney had encouraged him in its conduct and maintenance.

Soon after the publication of these statements the District-Attorney requested us to send for the author of them and ascertain their truth or falsity, a request which we were not slow to grant, inasmuch as the District-Attorney is the legal adviser of the Grand Jury, and necessarily brought into daily association with it.

We therefore caused to attend and be examined before us the author of the statements in question, and all other persons who could throw light on their truth or falsity, and, after a thorough investigation, desire to present to the court as follows:

We find the author of the charges had no evidence

upon which to base them, except alleged newspaper reports, which in the form published had no foundation in fact.

We find that no request was ever made to the District-Attorney to supply the Grand Jury with any evidence in the matter named, and that upon the trial of the indictment the District-Attorney presented to the court evidence collected wholly by himself, and that a conviction was obtained by him without reference to the testimony taken before the Grand Jury.

We desire further to express our disapproval and condemnation of unfounded charges of this character, which, whatever may be the motive in uttering them, can only serve to create a feeling of unwarranted distrust in the minds of the community with regard to the integrity of public officials, and tends only to hinder the prompt administration of justice.

Dated New York, February 29, 1892.

  (Signed)  HENRY S. HERRMAN, *Foreman.*

D. W. O'HALLORAN, *Secretary.*

After the Grand Jury's presentment Judge Martine made a statement, of which the following is a copy:

Mr. Foreman and Gentlemen of the Grand Jury:

It is gratifying indeed to find that your body has seen fit to make some investigation of the attack, such as was made in the public press by a certain gentleman in this community. Coming, as it does, from a clergyman, coming from one who naturally, from his calling, has some standing and repute in this community, it is quite natural that some credence should be given to the statement, and quite fair to assume that a person of that character would not make any unwarranted and unfounded attacks, and the public might assume that there was some basis for the attack, or was at the time it was made, when it had gained such publicity in the public press.

It was an attack upon the officials in this community. An attack of this character has the effect usually to bring officials into contempt and into disrepute, but when it is suggested that they are guilty of malfeasance and misconduct in office, and suggested that they failed to discharge the duties of office, and had gone a step further, to refuse to aid or assist those who wanted to bring about an investigation of crime, then it becomes a serious accusation calling for an investigation by such a body as yours.

After the first inquiry—after the first suggestion of official inquiry—the people came to comprehend that there was no foundation for the accusation, and it is indeed gratifying to find that after your investigation there was nothing but rumor, nothing but hearsay, to base any accusation upon. It is an easy matter to bring a public officer into disrepute, and then a difficult matter for a public officer to reinstate himself in the confidence of the public. Gentlemen, in this case I think you have done what you should have done. The District-Attorney of this county was your legal adviser. You confined your examination as to an investigation of the attacks made against him.

The person who made the accusations against him must have some reason of his own ; either a desire for public notoriety, or he may have believed it might result in some general good, or what not—what his motives may have been I can't say ; but it may well seem, a person occupying his station, a person in his calling, should be careful before making such an accusation unless he had some just foundation for it.

The foregoing from the Grand Jury and from the Bench was intended as a quietus, and was so interpreted by the City Officials, by Tammany Hall, and by the public journals published in its interests. Brief editorial extracts from half a dozen or so of such journals, are the following :

"The best employment to which the Rev. Dr. Parkhurst can now devote himself is prolonged prayer and repentance to atone for the grievous sin of which he has been guilty. An appropriate place wherein to give him the opportunity to subject himself to such spiritual mortification would be a penitentiary cell."

"It appears now, however, that the Rev. Dr. Parkhurst is the sort of clergyman with which the public has been already too familiar in times past; a kind of political pulpiteer who pounds 'the pulpit, drum ecclesiastic,' for the sake of filling the public ear and drawing a big audience, or congregation as he would call it, to his discourses. This takes the place of inspiration from the Bible and the ministerial work of 'bringing sinners to repentance,' and the result of it would be, in any event, to bring the pulpit into contempt."

"We presume that New York is governed about as badly as the other cities of the State, and that is saying a great deal; but it cannot be governed as badly as certain metropolitan papers represent, unless New

York is a community of idiots and criminals. When we see in a New York newspaper a long list of men, responsible for the government of the city, with charges appended to the name of each varying from murder in the first degree to larceny from the person, we no longer shudder at the awfulness of the exposition; we laugh at its absurdity."

"These well-meaning people who go off half cocked are a terror and a stumbling-block to every good cause. They hastily generalize, make rash and reckless statements and then are compelled to eat their words. They make themselves ridiculous and their future utterances are discounted about fifty per cent."

"It was this sort of thing that misled Dr. Parkhurst. He no doubt meant well. He saw certain grave charges in the public prints against the integrity of city officials, and believed it to be his duty as a minister to start a crusade. But the specific charges he made, on newspaper evidence, were baseless, and his crusade turns out a fiasco."

It was while matters were in this troubled condition (on the very day in fact, that the Presentment against me was adopted), that, in company with Mr. Moss, counsel for the Society for the Prevention of Crime, and Frank Lewis, our detective, I visited the District-Attorney at his office and asked him to aid me in bringing a number of excise cases before the Grand Jury. These cases, six or seven in number, which had been prepared with a good deal of care, were against liquor-dealers who were known to have a good deal of "pull" with the authorities, and whom therefore, it was presumable, neither the District-Attorney nor the Police Justices would jump at the chance of inconveniencing or convicting. The names of these liquor-dealers were furnished us by a gentleman who, although in close intimacy with many members of the organization we were fighting, has, nevertheless, been in constant and silent alliance with ourselves, and to whom we have now for nearly three years been under continuous obligation. Indeed it may here be remarked that a part, at least, of the accuracy and assurance with which we have been able to speak touching the condition of the Police Department and the Municipal Administration, is due to the testimony of parties who were either close to Tammany or even inside of it, but who secretly desired its overthrow.

But to return to our excise cases. It made very little difference to us whether we were able to obtain conviction or not; cases of this kind were certain to win publicity through the press; and the more conspicuous the case, if only our proofs were not at fault, the greater would be the effect produced upon the popular mind if the case went against us: for from first to last our object has not been to convict criminals so much as to convince the public that under the existing condition of things, criminals run little or no risk of being convicted.

It was a Monday morning that we three went into

the attorney's office. On entering, there was precipitated a condition of awkwardness in which there were combined in about equal degree, elements of the sublime and the ridiculous. Without any excessive display of hospitality on his part, but with his eyes glued upon me with an expression of amusement and displeasure, I approached the District-Attorney saying :

"'Mr. District-Attorney, the report has emanated from your office two or three times lately that you find it difficult to procure evidence sufficient to convict in cases of violation of the excise laws, etc. Now, we should love to be of assistance to you, and I have with me a number of cases of violations that occurred yesterday upon which we have secured important evidence. I am here to ask if you will be so kind as to bring us before the Grand Jury this morning and give us an opportunity to present these cases to them.'

"The District-Attorney said in reply :

"'Dr. Parkhurst, I refuse to have any official communication with you till you have withdrawn the falsehoods that you have spoken against me from your pulpit.'

"I said to him, 'That being the case I will ask our counsel, Mr. Moss, to confer with you in my stead,' and put in Mr. Moss's hands the list of cases, with the request that he should turn them over to Mr. Nicoll. He did so. Mr. Nicoll glanced at them, gave them back to Mr. Moss, saying that he did not care to keep them, that he would see that we came before the Grand Jury and that they could do with the cases as they liked."

I have been thus explicit in the recital of this scene for the reason that so much hung upon it. There were two attitudes which Mr. Nicoll might have assumed: he could have done precisely the thing that he did do, avail of the resources of his office to embarrass the efforts that were being made to secure the enforcement of law ; or he could have jumped to the altitude of his opportunity and said : " Yes, Dr. Parkhurst ; your object is identical with that of this office. You are jealous for the enforcement of law, and so are we. Anything that we can do to strengthen your hands shall be done. I will do all I can to make access to the Grand Jury easy and satisfactory to you and to your Society." Had Nicoll taken that attitude, the probability is that little more, comparatively speaking, would have have been heard of our movement. The victory which we have gained has not been gained so much by our fighting as by the injudicious precipitancy with which our movement has been opposed. Like a bird, we slid up on the wind that was blowing in our faces. If Nicoll had known that morning, what kind of stuff the Society for the Prevention of Crime was made of, and had had five minutes to recover from the personal prostration from which, since the 14th of February he had been suffering, his native shrewdness would have gained the better of his personal pique and he would have seized the opportunity and thrown me.

# CHAPTER V

### COLLECTING EVIDENCE

THE charges made from my pulpit on the 14th of February I was unable, at that time, to substantiate. They were founded on rumor. I was twitted upon that fact from the District-Attorney's office, the Grand-Jury room, and the Judge's bench. Probably not one of those who made official jest of my discomfiture but knew that all which I charged was true, and that if I had charged a great deal more, it would have been equally true. That, however, did not at all help the Society for the Prevention of Crime or its cause. There were only two alternatives open; either the battle must stop where it was, or I must be able to say "I know." The challenge had been thrown down, and I must either pick it up or allow the cause to go by default.

The power to stand up and say "I know" would have to be earned by a tour of personal inspection, and how much that means it is not part of our present purpose to relate, save to say that it afforded confessed enemies a point of assault, and gave to doubting friends material for no end of misgiving.

It has been said that it would have served the same purpose if the work had been done by the Society's detectives,—a position which we blankly deny. It is an incontrovertible fact that the statement of a paid detective is always discounted. No matter what his history and antecedents may have been, his salaried evidence is taken with an allowance. It is argued that such a tour of inspection was itself degrading, and it ought, for that reason, to have been made by my agents. It was against objections and criticisms of this kind that I published, through the columns of the newspapers, an address to the citizens of New York City, under date of April 13th, 1892, and it will be proper to insert extracts from that address at this point.

"I regret the egotism that seems involved in presuming to address so broad a readership. I trust, however, that I shall be acquitted of any presumptuous intention, more especially, as up to this time I have not penned a single word, either in acknowledgment of the support that has been accorded me, or in reply to the criticisms that have been passed upon me.

"Even now my object is not so much to defend the methods which I have seen it wise to adopt, as to put in distinct shape the one object toward which I am working, whether as preacher or as President of the Society for the Prevention of Crime.

"In the sermon which was preached from my pulpit

on the 14th of February last, the one point urged was that one of the greatest difficulties which the church has to encounter in the prosecution of its work is the license which is municipally allowed to vice. This was immediately met on the part of municipal authorities with a tempest of raillery which culminated in the presentment of the February Grand Jury. I was told that my charges were general, that I had no idea what I was talking about, and that the whole tendency of such vituperation was to bring the government into disgrace. . . .

"The evidence which, with the aid of detectives and friends, I was easily able to collect, was secured with the distinct end of showing, by unimpeachable testimony, something of the extent, infamy, and publicity of certain crimes, with the necessary inference that if a police force as competent as ours is conceded to be, and in the possession of all those legal powers known to be accorded to it, fails to hold such crimes in stern check, it can only be because of having entered into some evil alliance with them. It was not at all a matter between me and any individual parties. When I went before the Grand Jury with two hundred and eighty-four affidavits I said, 'Gentlemen, I have no interest in the conviction of these parties. Evidence has not been secured against them for the sake of inducing you to indict them. My object has been solely to secure in the general mind an indictment against the Police Department.'

"As to criticisms that have been passed, even by my friends, I want to say that I give them full credit for sincerity in all their strictures. At the same time it is always to be remembered that it is a thousand times easier to criticise another's action than it is to take action one's self, and if while I was planning how I could do something to help the cause some one else had devised a better method than the one I was working out, I am sure I should have been only too happy to strike into it, and work at his side and under his lead.

"It is claimed that work of so dirty a character I ought to have hired some one to do for me. I loathe the suggestion and I loathe the craven spirit that prompts it. If it was vicious in me to visit those places myself it would have been equally vicious, with an added element of damnable cowardice, to get some one to do it for me. No such system of ethics as that has either the moral vigor or the intellectual acumen to bore into the heart of existing corruption."

The first point to prove, then, was that criminal practices were being conducted throughout the town in a manner of outrageous openness that afforded *prima facie* evidence that there was collusion between police and criminals. Individual criminals, as such, we had no interest in. We were neither trying to convict them, nor were we any more trying to convert them. Naturally, the criminals became our enemies, and continued so until our real intent was understood. Just as naturally the Police Justices, the Police Commissioners, and the Superintendent of Police, together with their journalistic representatives, lost no opportunity to taunt us with having substituted the courtroom for the Bible and hymn-book in our contention with the fallen and the unfortunate. Divver, Byrnes, Martin and Sheehan knew exactly as well then as they do to-day that our attack was upon them, and not upon the petty criminals within their respective dioceses; and their voluminous discharge of hypocritical drivel had no other object than to confuse the issue and discredit the Society and myself, its representative. Our work, then, was not upon the bawdy-house, but upon the Tammany Police Department, through the bawdy-house; and in spite of the Commissioners, the Superintendent, and the Captains, we have won.

The necessity for such a tour of observation was, to my mind, so transparently necessary that it did not seem advisable to seek any considerable amount of counsel upon the matter. I conferred repeatedly with Mr. David J. Whitney, who was one of the most aggressive members of the Society, and who, through long warfare with the evil geniuses of our city, had made himself an expert in all that concerned the Society's work. He was a man who was very quick in his judgments, but exceedingly liable to be right. He agreed with me that there would be tremendous advantage in being able to speak of the city from out of my own personal acquaintance with it, but omitted no pains to convince me of the poisoned arrows of malignity to which I should be exposed if I made the venture. Having decided that destiny was a thing from which there is no escape, it remained to find a safe and congenial spirit whom I could take as my companion. More hinged upon this matter than I could then distinctly foresee ; it was necessary that such companion should be a man of unimpeachable personal character, and of an established position in community. Of course it was necessary, also, that he should undertake the work not out of any hasty or uncertain impulse, but purely out of devotion to the cause which the work represented.

While this matter was still being considered, I was called upon one evening, early in March '92, by a young man who had recently become a member of my congregation, and whom I had noticed in the church, but whom I had never personally met. Whether he had divined what was in my own mind, I do not know to this day, but he said that he had come to tell me that if there was anything he could do to assist me in the enterprise recently undertaken, he was unreservedly at my service. My good friend John Langdon Erving little realized all that was involved in his noble offer, or all that it was going to cause him in the way of criticism and obloquy before his heroic service was completed ; but suffice it to say that his offer of assistance was accepted and a general plan of operations outlined that same evening. I cannot let this opportunity pass of rendering to my friend Erving the tribute of my gratitude. If in connection with this whole warfare there have been words of invective and insinuations too dastardly and devilish to be forgiven, either in this world or the world to come, they were words that were spoken upon Erving. His was the manly stuff, however, that took no detriment from calumny, and I can speak no larger word of him than to say that without him, or a man as strong and noble-spirited as he, the efforts initiated in the spring of '92 must have issued in failure.

Of course, I have no purpose of publishing here the details of those three weeks which, in the company of Erving and under the guidance of detective Charles W. Gardner, I spent in traversing the avenues of our municipal hell. The details have been given to the public through the press, and by no journal more prolifically or with more of zest than by the one that has affected the deepest anguish at the vast number of pure minds that have been sullied by the repulsive disclosures.

Nevertheless, in full view of all that has passed, and in spite of all in the way of vicious criticism and honest misunderstanding that has ensued, I still am obliged to say that the course I took was the only course that could have been taken; and that under the like circumstances I would repeat precisely the same policy. No rhetoric that I might have availed of, and no theories of the situation that I might have promulgated, would ever have begun to take the place of my being able to say "I know." I may be permitted to say that when I stood in my pulpit shortly after, and on the strength of my own personal knowledge repeated in more of detail the charges for which I had just been "presented," I felt, clear to the centre of my being, that I was in a position from which no District-Attorney, no Grand Jury, and no Justice Martine, or any of his ilk, could ever shake me.

There is one feature of our tour of inspection that has not, perhaps been sufficiently indicated. We entered no houses that were not easy of access ; we were not trying to prove the existence of evil resorts, but were seeking to connect the police with those resorts by showing the fearless and flagrant way in which they were being run. We went into no places that were not recognized as notorious ; into no places that were not perfectly known by the patrolman on the beat, provided only he knew anything that was on his beat. Indeed our great anxiety, particularly after it began to be rumored that I was engaged in this investigation, was lest, in protection of their criminal interests, the police should arrange to raid some such resort while our visit upon it was in progress. In fact, almost the last and one of the vilest dens I entered was visited by the policeman while we were still in the house, and when we descended the steps he was standing guard over it. A while subsequent to this, and in another part of the town, a gentleman who was in our interest, in order to satisfy himself of the personal understanding existing between the police and criminal resorts, accepted the offer of a patrolman to stand as sentinel at the front door so long as he should remain in, and until he reappeared. The policeman did so. Because of the connection of the madame of that house with the Gardner case, our friend suggested to the patrolman that the notoriety of the place would make it a dangerous one to enter. The blue-coat said, " Not at all." It was then that our friend asked him if he would be so good as to keep guard over the house during his visit there, so as to notify him in case there should be signs of a raid. "Certainly," said our observant guardian of the public peace.

And we made it our purpose not only to visit places that were run with a vicious flagrancy that proved police connivance, not to say protection, but to acquaint ourselves with the very worst thing that was to be known and seen. If the thing was to be done it was going to be done thoroughly; or, to use the illustration employed by Judge Noah Davis a few weeks later, if I had got to enter hell, I was going to find its most hellish spot. My constant instruction to Gardner was, "Take me to the most notorious resort you know of." There had been dens of even more nefarious character than any we visited, worse than anything hinted at in the first chapter of Romans or mentioned in connection with Gomorrah ; but they were not open in March of 1892—if they had been we should have visited them. Having settled in my own mind my policy of action, the depth and foulness of the path over which the pursuance of that policy would lead me ceased to be an element in the question.

## CHAPTER VI

### AFFIDAVITS IN THE PULPIT

INTIMATION had been given that the gauntlet thrown down by the February Grand Jury would be taken up by us in my pulpit on the morning of March 13th. The ordinary furniture of the pulpit, in the shape of Bible and Hymn-books, was on that occasion supplemented by a copious package of affidavits. The discourse was preached from the text, "The wicked walk on every side, when the vilest men are exalted" (Psalm xii. 8), and with few modifications was as follows :

It will be well for us—you and me—to come to a full and frank understanding with each other, at the very threshold of our discussion this morning, as to the true scope of the campaign in which we are engaged, and in which, unless all signs are misleading, the hearts of increasing numbers are day by day becoming enlisted. What was spoken from this pulpit four weeks ago was spoken with a distinct intent, from which we have not in the meantime swerved, and from which we do not in coming time propose to swerve, whatever in the way of obstruction, vituperation, or intimidation may be officially or unofficially launched against us : for the one exclusive aim of the movement is to probe, to characterize, and to lay bare the iniquity that municipally antagonizes and neutralizes the efforts which a Christian pulpit puts forth to make righteousness the law of human life, individually, socially, and civilly. So that I apprehend my function as a preacher of righteousness as giving me no option in the matter. It is not left for me to say whether I shall do it or shall not do it, but to go straightway about my business without fear or favor.

It is important to recognize just here the purely moral intention of the crusade as security against its becoming complicated with considerations that stand aloof from the main point. A great many civic efforts have been made here and elsewhere that have resulted in nothing, for the single and sufficient reason that they have been side-tracked, switched off on to some collateral issue, mortgaged to some competitive interest. Suggestions, insinuations, criticisms that have reached me from various sources, some through the press, some through personal correspondence, make it incumbent upon me to declare that what has been said, and what will continue to be said, proceeds in no slightest degree from sympathy with or interest in any specific policy, whether political, reformatory, or religious, looking to the reconstruction of our municipal life.

I do not speak as a Republican or a Democrat, as a Protestant or a Catholic, as an advocate of prohibition, or as an advocate of license. I am moved, so help me Almighty God, by the respect which I have for the Ten Commandments, and by my anxiety as a preacher of Jesus Christ, to have the law of God regnant in individual and social life ; so that I antagonize our existing municipal administration, because I believe, with all the individual exceptions frankly conceded four weeks ago, that administration to be essentially corrupt, interiorly rotten, and in all its combined tendency and effect to stand in diametric resistance to all that Christ and a loyally Christian pulpit represent in the world.

Now there is another diversion, side-tracking device, that has been operated and that has been operated industrially, and which, as it seems to me, has had for its object to confuse the general mind, and so to break the force of the indictment made here four weeks ago. I refer, of course, to the presentment made by the February Grand Jury. In that presentment the substance of the censure passed upon the offending clergyman was that he uttered charges against an official founded upon newspaper reports. Why, I said at the time that it was founded upon newspaper report. So far as related to the McGlory matter, it was a hypothetical accusation and was exhibited as a hypothetical accusation. If the papers which published the story at the time, and which, so far as I could learn, had remained for six weeks uncontradicted, misrepresented the case, why then my accusation, so far as related to the McGlory matter, tumbled with it, and that is all of it involved in the very terms in which I then recognized the newspapers as my authority. If I had failed to indicate my authority, or if I had failed to indicate that so far as it related to the McGlory business, my charges stood or fell with that authority, the case would have been different; but, as it is, there seems to be in the action of the Grand Jury a lack of that frankness which I certainly had a right to expect, and which my own entire frankness in the Grand Jury room has certainly entitled me to receive.

The natural, not to say the intended, effect of the form under which the presentment was made, was to produce upon the minds of such as were not knowing to the very phraseology which I used, the impression that I had been stating, as of my own personal knowledge, matters which, upon a little sifting, disclosed themselves to have reached me only through the avenue of the press. I cannot feel that to be just. Nor can I otherwise interpret it than as calculated to represent as ministerial effusiveness and carelessness, that which had not an element of extravagance in it, and in that way covertly to impeach and bring into discredit my arraignment in its other details. Leaving that point, I would like merely to interpolate the inquiry, Why was it that an accusation that for six weeks had been lying unregarded and untouched in the public prints was at once made a subject of judicial investigation and carried to the point of presentment when reproduced in the pulpit?

But all that one side, and I am sorry to have asked you to devote a single moment's thought to a matter that has, to such a degree, the appearance of being personal to myself. All that aside, you will remember that the substance of the charge that four weeks ago was brought against a certain official, was that he betrayed a languid interest in the conviction of violators of law and allowed other considerations to intervene between himself and his official obligations. Now, that last is exactly what he has done in my own person since then. I went to him with business that pertained to his own department, and he peremptorily refused to hold official communication with me. His feelings toward me personally prevented his fulfilling the obligations due from him officially. Now, there is no newspaper rumor about that. I speak that I do know, and testify that which I have seen, and two witnesses are ready to bear their testimony to the fact. I am a citizen and a taxpayer, and I am refused audience with an officer whose salary I, as a taxpayer, am helping to pay, and whose services as an attorney I am entitled to avail of.

So far as that concerns me personally, of course I care nothing about it. It would be as childish as it would be wicked to bring into the pulpit personal differences as such. But the point is that, in the transaction just referred to, I, as a citizen, could get nothing from an officer of the Government, because, forsooth, I was not "solid" with him.

Now that is the genius of the entire Tammany business. You cannot get anything from Tammany unless you are "solid" with Tammany. A man, though he may be working night and day for the ennoblement and purification of the city he loves, has no rights which Tammany is bound to respect. We are obliged and glad to make all possible exceptions, and there are many such; but the fact is that Tammany, taken as a whole, is not so much a political party as it is a commercial corporation, organized in the interest of making the most possible out of its official opportunities, so that what the rest of us get from Tammany we have to get by fighting for it or paying for it. All of which is stated with enviable conciseness and frankness in the last number of the *North American Review*, in which the writer says:

"Tammany is no party and refuses allegiance to any. It has no principles or platforms to pledge it to duty. It fights only for itself. Its governmental theory is simple. It counts absolutely on the ignorance, the venal and depraved voters, holding them with the adhesive and relentless grasp of an octopus. It never alienates the grogshop keepers, the gamblers, the beer dealers, the nuisance makers, or the proletariat. Patriotism and a sense of duty count for nothing in its estimate of political forces. Party passion, selfishness, and hopes of victory and spoils are its supreme reliance."

And not only does the organization just referred to stand as the organization of crime, but it embodies the tyranny of crime. There are citizens in this town abominating the whole system that do not dare to stand up and be counted. One of the most striking features of the immense number of letters of thanks and encouragement that I have been receiving during the last four weeks is the large percentage written by people who did not dare to append their own signatures—distinctly in sympathy with everything that is true and pure and honest, and yet afraid over their own names to put into black and white their sincere views of a government whose duty it is to foster virtue, not drive it into hiding.

I do not refer to this for the purpose of charging the writers with cowardice. I only adduce the fact as demonstration of the inherent tyranny of the civilized brigands who are despotizing over us. Only in that connection I want to say that now is a good time to speak out; an excellent opportunity for moral heroism to come to the front and assert itself. Nothing frightens so easily as vice. "The wicked flee when no man pursueth," and they make still better time when somebody is pursuing. Time and time again during the past weeks, as I have, between the hours of 12 and 3 in the morning, sat in the company of women of a class almost too disreputable to be even named in this presence, I have heard the same thing said, that there is not much doing just now for the reason that everybody is scared. Some things have come, and they have a shrewd presentiment that more of the same sort is on the way. The scattering feathers and the plaintive peepings indicate that the shots are striking into the quick.

I cannot too strongly emphasize the fact, even at the risk of being repetitious, that my interest in this thing is due solely to the obstruction that such a condition of affairs puts upon my work as a preacher of righteousness. You cannot have men even of tainted reputation, saying nothing of character, high in municipal authority without that fact working the discouragement of virtue and the reduction of moral standards. It is a pretty trying state of affairs for such as are attempting to improve the moral condition of our young men, in particular, to have officials high in power against whom the most damning and excoriating thing that can be done is to publish their history. A while ago the treasurer of a certain bank downtown, who was not even suspected of being dishonest, but whose name, through no fault of his own, had become associated with a disreputable firm, was thrown out of his position. The reason stated by the directors was, that while they cordially and unanimously recognized the integrity of the treasurer, they could not afford to jeopardize the interest of the bank by having associated with them a man that was tainted even to the slight degree of being mentioned in connection with dishonest dealing.

Now, that is the way you run a bank. That is the style of condition that you impose upon candidates for positions of financial trust. I am not here to criticise these conditions. But when you come to run a city, with a million and a half of people, with interests that are a great deal more than pecuniary, and a city, too, that is putting the stamp of its character or of its infamy upon every city the country through, then you have not always shrunk from putting into positions of trust men that are ex-dive-keepers and crooks and ex-convicts, and men whose detailed written history would draw tremblingly near to the verge of obscene literature.

The charge has been brought that the kind of discourse that was given here four weeks ago was entirely general, and was not characterized by that definiteness, or by that sharpness of detail that would commend it to the interest or the confidence of a judicial mind. Now, details, I confess, were the last things that I supposed that the virtuous people of this city would need, or that the administration of this city would want. It was with some surprise, therefore, that I understood that it was officially stated in the Stevenson "Slide" case that while ministers like myself were willing enough to sit in their own houses and vituperate the city government, it was impossible to get them to procure evidence that would help to convict suspects of violation of laws. As I say, this was something of a surprise, for while I knew that the city government had allowed the ladies to teach them how to sweep the streets, I did not imagine it would be considered a part of my ministerial duty to go into the slums and help catch the rascals, especially as the police are paid nearly five million dollars a year for doing it themselves. But it is never to late to broaden your diocese. I, therefore, selected seven names of parties that I imagined might occasionally forget themselves and be guilty of the violation of the Excise law, put evidence-takers on their track, and having secured evidence such as my counsel deemed sufficient, met the District-Attorney in the interview above described.

Opportunity of official intercourse being denied me (I omitted just now to mention the fact that the seven names selected were of parties that are way up in the confidences of Tammany councils), opportunity of official intercourse being denied me, my lawyer put the names of the parties before the District-Attorney, which he politely returned, and said that we could take them before the Grand Jury and that he would secure us the opportunity. I was admitted to the Grand Jury, but upon stating my errand was courteously informed that attending to such matters was not exactly in their line, and was invited to move on, and first try my luck with the police court. Application was therefore made to the police court, and warrants were obtained. That was the first gleam of hope that broke upon us, and down to date it is the last gleam. The case was put over to last week,

Monday. On Monday we all gathered again at the Tombs, counsel and witnesses, only to have the Judge tell us that we could come again this week, Tuesday. I said four weeks ago that our municipal administration showed a languid interest in the conviction of criminals. I was taunted with dealing in generalities. Now there is a specification, seven of them. Go put them along with the Grand Jury's presentment.

Well, the work of gathering evidence, thus begun, grew upon me in interest and fascination. Last Sunday, therefore, while we were quietly studying and praying over the matter of Foreign Missions, I had a force of five detectives out studying up city missions, and trying to discover whether the Police Department shows any practical respect to its obligation to enforce the excise laws on the Sabbath.

Before going on with that I want to mention a singular little episode that also occurred last Sabbath on the east side. The story met my eye in the morning papers and I asked a legal friend to go to the clerk of the court and verify it, which he did in its essential features. A policeman on Division Street, urged thereto, so the story runs, by the necessity that he felt himself under just at this time of showing the community what a lively interest the police take in preserving the holy quiet of the Lord's Day, went into an open grocer's shop and arrested the shopkeeper for selling a three-cent cake of soap. Now I do not want to be understood as condoning that offence.

Cleanliness is next to godliness, but cleanliness isn't godliness, and I am not here to criticise Judge Kilbreth, in whose integrity I have thorough reason to put confidence, for putting the offender under bail to appear before the General Sessions. But while this three-cent soap transaction was transpiring there were a good many other things transipring, and I return to the experience of my five detectives.

I have here the results of their day's work, neatly typewritten, sworn to, corroborated, and subject to the call of the District-Attorney. There is here the list of parties that last Sunday violated the ordinance of Sunday closing. One of these covers the east side and the other the west side of town. These names are interesting, some of them especially so, from one cause or another—in some instances on account of their official position, either present or recent; in other cases because of their family connection or intimacies with the powers that be. These lists include violations in twenty-two precincts. The statement sworn to is the following, omitting the names and addresses of the witnesses, which are in the documents, of course, given in full: "John Smith, of such a street and number, in said city, being duly sworn, deposes and says, that at the city of New York, on Sunday, March 6, 1892, between the hours of 8 A. M. and 12 P. M., deponent, in company with one John Jones, visited the following liquor saloons where wine or malt or spirituous liquors were exposed for sale; that there were people drinking at the bars of all these places, to wit.:"

Then follows the list of places, with addresses, and the number of people present in each. Then comes John Jones's sworn corroborations of John Smith's affidavit. In other words "legal evidence," which is what I understand our municipal administration desires to have this pulpit furnish it. Of course, I am not going to take up your time by reading the names. Only a little in the way of recapitulation, for illustration's sake. Second Precinct, 7 saloons open, 55 people present; Fourth Precinct, 10 saloons open, 45 people present; Fourteenth Precinct, 15 saloons open, 169 people present; Nineteenth Precinct (that is ours), 18 saloons open, 205 people present. In all (I do not mean all the saloons that were open, but all the open ones that our detectives happened to strike), in all, 254 saloons, 2,438 people present. They don't want "generalities," they want particularities. Well, there are 254 of them, not pulpit grandiloquence, nor ministerial exuberance, but hard, cold affidavits. If the concerned guardians of the public peace and the anxious conservators of municipal laws want facts we will guarantee to grind them out a fresh grist every blessed week. Now, let them take vigorous hold of the material furnished above, or quit their hypocritical clamoring after specific charges.

It has seemed to me that there would be a peculiar propriety in studying a little way into the general trend of things in the Nineteenth Precinct, as that is the one in which our own church is situated, and from which we draw the major part of our congregation. To this end I have had during the last few days a number of interested people, some of them paid detectives, some of them volunteers from this congregation, scouring the ground with a view to learning something about the gambling-houses and the houses of a disorderly character. A gambler who is a dealer in one of the faro banks here told one of our party that the small games were running pretty quiet now because Dr. Parkhurst's society (the Society for the Prevention of Crime) had so frightened the police that they had made the gamblers close up for a time, till this thing should blow over. I only mention that that you may get at the true inwardness of the situation. The police can stop gambling just the instant that they conclude that it is unsafe not to. They will go just as far as the exigencies of the case push them, and to all appearances not a step farther.

Among places of this character reported to me are two that are possessed of a melancholy interest, because of the youthful character of the patrons—a gambling house a little above 40th street, furnished with roulette, hazard, and red and black tables, in which there were counted forty-eight young men, and a policy shop, three blocks above our church, running full blast, and which forty young men were seen to enter last Tuesday.

Leaving the gambling-house for the present, I must report to you what was discovered in a region of iniquity that in this presence will have to be dealt with with as much caution and delicacy as the nature of the subject will allow. I have here a list of thirty houses, names and addresses, all specified, that are simply houses of prostitution, all of them in this precinct. These thirty places were all of them visited by my friend, or my detective, on the 10th and also on the 11th of March, and solicitations received on both dates. I spent an hour in one of these places myself, and I know perfectly well what it all means, and with what entire facility such houses can be gotten into. That house is three blocks only from the spot where I am standing now. All of this has been neatly typewritten, sworn to, corroborated, and is subject to the call of the District-Attorney.

And now, fathers and mothers, I am trying to help your sons. From the very commencement of my ministry here I confess that to be of some encouragement and assistance to young men has been my great ambition. Appeal after appeal has come to me these last four weeks, signed " A Father " or " A Mother," begging me to try to do something for their dear boys. But, as things are, I do declare there is not very much that I can do for them. I never knew till within three weeks how almost impossible it is for a young man to be in the midst of the swim of New York City life, under present conditions, and still be temperate and clean. I had supposed that the coarse, bestial vices were fenced off from youthful contact with some show at least of police restriction. So far as I have been able to read the symptoms of the case, I don't discover the restrictions. There is little advantage in preaching the Gospel to a young fellow on Sunday if he is going to be sitting on the edge of a Tammany-maintained hell the rest of the week.

Don't tell me I don't know what I am talking about. Many a long, dismal, heart-sickening night, in company with two trusty friends, have I spent since I spoke on this matter before, going down into the disgusting depths of this Tammany-debauched town; and it is rotten with a rottenness that is unspeakable and indescribable, and a rottenness that would be absolutely impossible except by the connivance, not to say the purchased sympathy, of the men whose one obligation before God, men, and their own conscience is to shield virtue and make vice difficult. Now that I stand by, because before Almighty God, I know it, and I will stand by it though buried beneath presentments as thick as autumn leaves in Vallombrosa, or snowflakes in a March blizzard.

Excuse the personal reference to myself in all this, but I cannot help it. I never dreamed that any force of circumstances would ever draw me into contacts so coarse, so beastly, so consummately filthy as those I have repeatedly found myself in the midst of these last days. I feel as though I wanted to go out of town for a month to bleach the memory of it out of my mind, and the vision of it out of my eyes.

I am not ignorant of the colossal spasms of indignation into which the trustees of Tammany ethics have been thrown by the blunt and inelegant characterization of a month ago, and I have a clear, as well as a serene, anticipation of what I have to expect from the same sources for having deliberately sought out and entered into the very presence of iniquity in its vilest shape, for there is nothing in the first chapter of Romans, read this morning, that will outdo in filthiness the scenes which my eyes have just witnessed, and not till I look on the great White Throne can the foul traces of it be effaced; but horrible though the memory of it must always be to me, it has earned me a grip on the situation that I would not surrender for untold money. But the grim and desolate part of it all is that these things are all open and perfectly easily accessible. The young men, your boys, probably know that they are. Ten minutes of sly indoctrination, such as a tainted comrade might give them, would afford them all the information they would need to enable them with entire confidence to pick out either a cheap or an expensive temple of vile fascination, where the unholy worship of Venus is rendered. The door will open to him, and the blue-coated guardian of civic virtue will not molest him. I spent an hour in such a place yesterday morning, and when we came down the steps I almost tumbled over a policeman who appeared to be doing picket duty on the curbstone.

To say that the police do not know what is going on and where it is going on, with all the brilliant symptoms of the character of the place distinctly in view, is rot. I do not ask anyone to excuse or to apologize for my language. You have got to fit your words to your theme. We do not handle charcoal with a silver ladle nor carry city garbage out to the dumping ground in a steam-yacht. Anyone who, with all the easily ascertainable facts in view, denies that drunkenness, gambling, and licentiousness in this town are municipally protected, is either a knave or an idiot. It is one of the rules and regulations of the Police Department: "It is the duty of the Superintendent to enforce in the city of New York all the laws of the State and ordinances of the city of New York and ordinances of the Board of Health, and the rules and regulations of the Board of Police; to abate all gaming houses, rooms, and premises and places kept or used for lewd or obscene purposes, and places kept or used for the sale of lottery tickets or policies."

Another rule is: "Captains will be diligent in enforcing the laws relating to lotteries, lottery policies and shops; the selling of liquor and gambling of all kinds." Still another rule governing patrolmen is the following: "Patrolmen must carefully watch all disorderly houses or houses of bad fame within their post; observe by whom they are frequented and report their observations to the commanding officer." Still another : " Patrolmen shall report to their commanding officers all persons known or suspected of being policy dealers, gamblers, receivers of stolen property, thieves, burglars, or offenders of any kind." Again : " Each patrolman must by his vigilance render it extremely difficult, if not impossible, for any one to commit crime on his post." The obligations of our Police Department to enforce law are distinct, and their failure to do it is just as distinct.

I am not making the definite charge that this proceeds from complicity with violators of the laws, but I do make the distinct charge that it proceeds either from complicity or incompetency. They can take their choice. I do not believe, though, that any considerable number of people in New York consider them incompetent. This is disproved by the consummate ability with which certain portions of their official obligations are discharged, and by the complete success with which, when on one or two occasions they made up their minds, for instance, that the liquor saloons should be closed, they were closed up tight and dry, from Harlem to the Battery. Their ability I am willing to applaud indefinitely, knowing all the time, though, that the more I applaud them for their ability the more I damn them for their delinquency.

With the backing, then, of such facts legally certified to as have been presented this morning, we insist, in behalf of an insulted and outraged public, that the Police Department, from its top down, shall, without further shift or evasion, proceed with an iron hand to close up gambling-houses, houses of prostitution, and whiskey-shops open in illegal hours. If this is what they cannot do, let them concede the point, and give place to someone who can. If this is what they will not do, let them stand squarely on the issue and be impeached according to the provisions of the Code.

In a closing word, voicing the righteous indignation of the pure and honest citizenship of this tyrannized municipality, let me in a representative way say to Tammany: " For four weeks you have been wincing under the sting of a general indictment, and have been calling for particulars. This morning I have given you particulars, two hundred and eighty-four of them. Now, what are you going to do with them?"

We do not want to claim for the pulpit any position of advantage which does not belong to it, nor to speak in any manner arrogantly of its peculiar facilities of influence ; but we are probably correct in saying that the sermon above reproduced disturbed the enemy because it came, not from the newspaper, but from the pulpit. This is illustrated by the fact that the same criticism which I made against the District-Attorney had been previously made quite as well and fully as sharply by the press and had not been resented.

# CHAPTER VII

#### PRESENTMENT BY THE GRAND JURY AGAINST THE POLICE DEPARTMENT

TAMMANY HALL blackguarded me for preaching my sermon of February 14th because I indulged in generalities and spoke from hearsay; but that was not a circumstance to the way in which they blackguarded me for my sermon of March 13th, because I gave them particulars and spoke from personal knowledge. There is great difficulty in proceeding against criminals in a way that will exactly conform to their convenience or fall in with their æsthetic predilections. I cannot seem to hit upon any method of dealing with them that secures their cordial endorsement. The District-Attorney, who had made himself somewhat conspicuous by his disapprobation of my February policy, was equally hesitant about applauding my reverse policy of the month following. Being of a legal mind, it seemed as though he would be gratified by the particularity of my legally sustained charges; but at any rate he never gave me any indications of his gratification. Police Commissioner Martin was reported in a published interview as lamenting the effect that must have been produced upon the pure-hearted attendants at my church on the morning of March 13th. It is a touching token of that Commissioner's intrinsic delicacy of spirit that, having been so long a constituent element of a Police Department like ours, he should still have retained his innate sensitiveness and have experienced pain at the thought of the hypothetical "blush" of the members of my congregation.

These references have been made only as samples of the taciturn contempt with which Tammany received my bill of particulars, showing that the passion exhibited by them the month previous was due not to the fact that my charges were general and unsustained, but to the fact that anybody had dared to make any charges against them of any kind, sustained or unsustained, general or specific. In other words, all the threats, official and unofficial, that were flung at me on the occasion of my first sermon were simply parts of one stupendous game of bluff played in order to deter me and everyone else from doing anything more of the same sort.

Fortunately for the cause, however, the Grand Jury then sitting was of quite a distinct species from the Hermann and O'Halloran Jury of the month previous, and declined to be the tool of any District-Attorney or of any political interest. Our community, which is now rejoicing in the overthrow of Tammany Hall, has very little idea of the degree to which it is indebted for that overthrow, to the careful, faithful and heroic work done by the March Grand Jury of 1892. Its foreman was Henry M. Tabor; the other members were as follows :

David L. Einstein,               R. L. Sherman,
James Williams,                  Robert Rutter,
Nathan Farnbacher,               G. Foster,
George Harral,                   E. G. Bogert,
Wm. Lauterbach,                  C. E. Merrill,
T. J. Davis,                     Wm. Moir,
R. McCarrerty,                   Geo. Holbrook,
J. B. Bloomingdale,              F. Mead, Jr.,
A. G. Hyde,                      Wm. H. Marston,
G. E. Taintor,                   J. L. Hyde,
Andrew J. Fay,                   J. W. Tappin.

Foreman Tabor handled matters in a way to suit himself. That is to say, his experience as a juror had made him familiar with the fact that a Grand Jury does not fulfil its functions by playing tail to the District-Attorney's kite. It is an independent and irresponsible body, a Grand Jury is, and, properly speaking, no more the subject of the District-Attorney than it is of the court-house janitor — a fact, however, of which the District-Attorney appears often to take good care to have the minds of the jurors unsuspicious. It was some months before I learned that there was any way of getting before the Jury save by a preliminary wrestling match in the District-Attorney's office.

Mr. Tabor, then, let it be repeated, understood his

rights and duties too well to allow of any pranks being played upon him by the gentleman below stairs. His Jury, which was in session during the weeks following the delivery of my discourse of March 13th, promptly passed the following resolution :

"*Resolved*, That the District-Attorney be, and is hereby requested to produce all evidence before this Grand Jury regarding the cases referred to by Dr. Parkhurst and his associates and Society's agents, and request Dr. Parkhurst and his agents to appear before this Jury at the earliest practicable moment."

This request was immediately transmitted and promptly responded to by myself and agents of the Society, and indictments found against several of the parties in whose houses we had been during our tour of nocturnal visitation.

It will be well to state parenthetically that when the matter of finding such indictments was suggested by some members of the Jury, I stated that whether it was desirable for them to do so was a question for them to decide, but that that was a matter in which I personally, and as a representative of the Society for the Prevention of Crime had no interest; that we were not engaged in a crusade against disorderly houses but against the police considered as their presumed protectors ; but that the thing which would gratify us most, and meet what we considered the ends of justice, would be for them to push their inquiries to a point where they could see their way clear to formulate charges against the Police Department in its entirety. This was not said with any intention of dictating to the Jury its line of duty. We, however, wanted it understood that the object we, as a Society, had in view, was something far deeper than the suppression of any local outbreaks of crime, or of any individual violation of law. Whether this statement of our desire and purpose had any influence on the jurors is of no particular importance, but it is of importance to notice that the work which they did was thoroughly consistent with our own plan of campaign, and that the remainder of its time it occupied for the most part, not in indicting individual violators of gambling and excise laws, etc., but in prosecuting its inquiries into the matter of police negligence and criminality.

A considerable number of the higher officials of the Police Department were summoned before Mr. Tabor's Jury. As has since been so amply demonstrated, Police Commissioners, Superintendent, Inspectors, and Captains are a coy and innocent lot. They are so careful not to perjure themselves that they acquire a morbid distrust of their own memories, and for fear that they should say more than they can quite conscientiously take their oath upon, narrow their testimony down to a scope so narrow as to be practically valueless so far as relates to the securing of any material, or at least specific results. Another, although perhaps a less complimentary way of putting the same matter, would be to say, that the adroit officials declined to be snared in any of the nooses that Foreman Tabor threw to them, and returned to headquarters the same array of gold-banded innocence and brass-buttoned ingenuousness that they continued to be down to the later date of Mr. Goff's experiments upon them.

But although the Jury was unable, in the short time at its command, and in view of the unresponsive character of the witnesses upon which it was obliged to rely, to gather facts sufficient to warrant an indictment against any particular officer or officers, yet they discovered enough to justify their formulating charges against the Police Department as such, which were couched in the form of the following presentment:

*To the Honorable the Court of General Sessions and the Honorable the Recorder, Frederick Smyth:*

Owing to public and general charges having been made against the efficiency of the Police Department in suppressing vice and arresting law-breakers, this Grand Jury has spent considerable time in investigating these accusations.

It is conceded by all, that the Police Department is splendidly organized, and is not excelled in its ability to cope with crime. The comparative safety of travel and freedom from disorder on the streets are evidence of the ability of the force.

It must, however, be as fully conceded that certain

crimes, such as the maintaining of gambling-houses and disorderly houses, and the violation of excise law, are very prevalent, and that they are not seriously interfered with by the police.

The usual excuse is the difficulty of entrance into such places (although easily accessible to the public), and of procuring legal evidence. An investigation of the facts shows that few raids upon gambling and disorderly houses are made by the police of their own volition, and rarely, if ever, by the captain personally ; and in nearly all cases action is taken by private citizens or agents of societies upon which warrants are issued and raids made.

The police rules provide for regular reports by captains of police to headquarters of all gambling and disorderly houses in their precincts. Such reports are regularly made, and there is in Police Headquarters a long list of houses of that character, giving their exact location and the kind of business conducted in each of them.

Section 282 of the Consolidation Act requires the police to carefully observe and inspect all such premises, and to repress and to restrain all unlawful conduct in them, and gives them power to make arrests in such cases with or without warrants.

Section 285 of the Consolidation Act gives each policeman the power to report to the Superintendent any such premises, and to state the reasonable grounds for believing that the law is violated upon them, whereupon the Superintendent may issue his own warrant without any necessity of applying to a police justice, upon which warrant his officers may break into the suspected premises and arrest any persons found violating the law and capture any apparatus used in such unlawful business.

A large amount of testimony has been presented showing the existence and violation of law in large numbers of these places. The Grand Jury has indicted the proprietors of some of these places, and they have been arrested under such indictments and have pleaded. In these very cases further testimony has been presented showing that there was no abatement in these premises of the same disorderly practices, and that there was no appearance of police interference.

With the facts before us that these places do exist in large numbers, that they are well known to the police, that their locations and special lines of business are recorded by the Department, and that very particular and express duties are imposed by law upon the police to inspect and repress these places (Section 282), and that extraordinary powers of breaking into houses without previous application for judicial warrants are allowed to the police in order that they may perform such duties (Section 285), and with the fact that has plainly appeared to us that the police seldom use these powers, or even apply to magistrates for warrants to carry out their legal duties, there are presented to us the best reasons for condemning the inaction of the Police Department in these matters. They are either incompetent to do what is frequently done by private individuals with imperfect facilities for such work, or else there exist reasons and motives for such inaction which are illegal and corrupt. The general efficiency of the Department is so great that it is our belief that the latter suggestion is the explanation of the peculiar inactivity.

In reference to excise violations the proofs which have been produced, and our own observation clearly show that the existence of open saloons and the sale of liquor in them at unlawful hours is the general rule, and it is clear that there is very little attempt by the police to interfere with these practices.

The present situation certainly warrants the condemnation of the Police Department in the matters above mentioned. The force is paid liberally for the work of enforcing the law. They do enforce the law in many respects in a superior manner, but if they be permitted to discriminate in favor of certain forms of crime for reasons well known to themselves, there is no telling where the same course will lead them to, or leave the interests of our city. Circumstances and testimony offered have tended to show financial considerations in some cases for lax administration.

Indeed, the publicity with which the law is violated and the immunity from arrest enjoyed by the lawbreaker is inconsistent with any other theory. It is obvious that when a confession by a lawbreaker of payment for protection would subject him to penalties not only for his acknowledged crime but also for bribegiving, it is extremely difficult to collect trustworthy evidence in direct proof of such charges. It has been thought best at the present time to go no further than to make this general presentment, so that the courts and the residents of our city may be properly informed and warned against the dangerous evil that is in the midst of us.

The foregoing was unanimously adopted.

HENRY M. TABOR, *Foreman*.

GRAND JURY ROOM, March 31, 1892.

# CHAPTER VIII

### BYRNES AND THE "GREAT SHAKE-UP"

No one who is at all familiar with what preceded the action of the March Grand Jury, and what has transpired since that time, will be surprised at the space which we have devoted in Chapter VII. to the sessions of that Jury and to the presentment in which its painstaking investigations culminated. That presentment furnished us the groundwork on the basis of which all our subsequent efforts have been prosecuted to establish the legal credibility of our charges against the Police Department. The Jury published it as its sworn opinion that the police force of New York was either incompetent or criminal, and that it was not incompetent. So that from that time on, whenever we found it convenient or necessary to call our Police Department vicious, or to apply to it any other epithet that occasion seemed to require, we felt the combined judicial authority of the March Grand Jury as our voucher and guaranty; it lifted the activity of the Society for the Prevention of Crime out of the region of crankism, and wrought within that Society a grounded assurance and secured to it a dignity and a status. A great deal of the recent victory on the 6th of November was simply the action of the March Jury of 1892 come to its fruitage.

The decided terms in which the presentment was couched were received by the friends and officials of the Police Department with inexpressible scorn. The generality of the charges relieved specific pressure on individual members of the Department, but made it only by so much the more difficult either to reply to or to escape the suspicion beneath which all its members were henceforth obliged to labor. They were instantly converted into a body of suspects, and no language which they might employ, either of the ordinary or of the profane sort, operated to their relief or deliverance.

If the police officials had been as honest in their intention as they were jealous of their reputation, they would have taken prompt measures to follow up the presentment, and either have attempted to refute the imputation or purify the Department. But the second they did not want to do, and the first they knew they could not do. It is amusing at this later date, when so many of the foul secrets of the Police Commissioners and their subordinates have been brought to light by the Lexow Investigation, to recall the passionate declarations of innocence with which the hard, dry imputations of the March Grand Jury were greeted. Of course the Commissioners, the Superintendent, the

Inspectors, and the Captains knew then just as well as we know now, how inadequately even the stern language of Mr. Tabor's jurors was to state the whole foul truth of the case; and yet those same officials, some of whom are directing the affairs of the Department to-day, and even planning to have a hand in its reorganization, rose up in indignant protestation against the cruel injustice that had been done the "Finest Police Force in the World."

The *Tribune* of April 2d quoted Commissioner McClave as saying : " If my information is correct, the police power in this city is the best in the world." It will be remembered that this same Mr. McClave resigned his position on the Board shortly after Mr. Goff's interview with him before the Lexow Committee.

President Martin is quoted by the *World* of April 3d, as saying : " The accusation that the police are in the pay of disorderly and gambling-houses is both inconsistent and absurd."

Inspector Williams is quoted by the same authority as saying : " I have been a police officer for twenty-six years, and the Rev. Dr. Parkhurst and the members of his church have contributed more to houses of prostitution than I have, and have derived more benefits from them." Newspaper files of that date will furnish the interested inquirer with considerable material of the same quality.

The decided and confident terms in which the

presentment was couched produced throughout the city a strong reaction in behalf of our cause. Popular sentiment is a peculiar commodity, and rises and falls with an energy that it cannot always itself account for. There is a certain contagion in human opinion, and at the impulse of Foreman Tabor's manifesto, the human mind, as reflected by individual utterances and by the attitude of the press, arrayed itself unequivocally on the side of the new movement against the Police Department. We could distinctly see that a reactionary tendency would before long assert itself, and were not, therefore, surprised when it appeared. But, for the time being, the cause represented by the Society for the Prevention of Crime was in the ascendant, and the Police Department driven to the wall and obliged to make some show of virtue, however destitute it might be of virtue's reality. This astute commingling of the comic and tragic was consummated in what has since come to be known as the "Great Police Shake-up," and occurred on the 19th of April, 1892. Before entering into the particulars of the "Shake-up" it is necessary to notice that one week previous, that is, on April 12th, William Murray had resigned from the Superintendency of the Police, and had been succeeded by Chief-Inspector Thomas Byrnes.

Thomas Byrnes had won international reputation as a detective, and it was somehow hoped that what had evinced itself as ingenuity in his former capacity would reproduce itself in the shape of executive talent in the new and more authoritative position to which he was now promoted. No man ever had a greater opportunity to make himself felt, if only he had the requisite integrity of purpose and the requisite strength of purpose. The popular mind was aroused to the necessity of more thorough administration of the Department, and the moral sense of the town was prepared to extend to him a warm welcome and to afford him firm backing; and among all these there were none more ready to recognize any honest effort on Mr. Byrnes's part than the Society for the Prevention of Crime and its executive committee; and the daily journals of that date bear abundant testimony to the fact.

The prompt aggressive action of the Superintendent went far to strengthen the confidence that we were willing and anxious to repose in him. He not only stated that his " one supreme object would be the enforcement of the laws without fear or favor," but immediately bestirred himself in a way that strengthened the hopes of his friends, and excited the apprehension of evil-doers. The second day after his appointment the police captains were all of them summoned to his office. The *Recorder* of April 19th, reports him as declaring that he was " fully determined to enforce the laws. He had nothing to do with the making of the laws," he said, " but so long as they exist he would see that they were obeyed. The saloons would be closed down every Sunday while these laws were in force."

The degree to which the general expectation was aroused is indicated by the following extract from the *Herald* of April 16th :

The days of what few gambling-houses and disreputable resorts that are still open in the city are numbered. By the latter part of next week these will go the way of those already closed. Every police captain in the city has received instructions to arrest the proprietors of all such places, and to see that each and every house is immediately shut and barred. They have also received instructions to allow no violations of the Excise law, and every saloon-keeper who has heretofore obliged his thirsty patrons on Sunday morning will be arrested the moment his doors are opened.

His first Sunday in office only about half the usual number of saloons were reported to be open. No one could be at all knowing to the strength with which crime was intrenched among the criminal classes, and lawlessness become a chronic condition among the police, without anticipating that Mr. Byrnes could not carry out his professed intention without a struggle ; but we were all of us inclined for a few days to believe that he would make a brave fight of it, and we would have jumped in with him for all that we were worth.

This brings us again to the point which we have already touched on a previous page, namely, that of the " Shake-up." This took place just one week after

Mr. Byrnes became Superintendent; thirty-five captains were shifted. So complete an upheaval had never been known. This event, taken in connection with the "dry" Sunday, and the great show of purpose evinced during the previous week, made of the 19th of April a red-letter day.

It was not until there had been a little time for thought that even the most wary among us ventured to interpret the last move as being anything other than an honest attempt to strengthen the Department and purify its service. The Superintendent might transfer his captains every day now and nobody would be hoodwinked by it; but it was a new thing then, and we were not so accustomed to being fooled with. That was before the Department had done as much posing as it has since, and before it took as much police wool as it does now to overspread the public eye. One of the singular features in the history of the last three years, as far down as the 6th of November last, when Mr. Byrnes displayed spasmodic virtue and made special arrangements for securing an honest ballot, has been the readiness with which the public has consented to have its impaired confidence in police officials restored. Even the Executive Committee of the Society for the Prevention of Crime have once or twice come very near to being swamped in the general condition of bamboozlement. The administrative and executive heads of the Department, to say nothing of their subordinates, must have derived a great deal of sly entertainment from the credulity with which the Superintendent's bit of innutritious bait was, on the 19th of April, seized by the people and by the newspapers. Even at that time, however, the question was sometimes covertly raised, " If Captain Jones, for instance, performs the duties of his office in an incompetent or criminal way in the Eighth Precinct, how is his service to be permanently improved by being shifted to the Ninth Precinct? If he is an able and faithful officer he can do his best work where he is best acquainted, and if he is an incompetent and corrupt officer, he cannot do good service anywhere." This view of the matter was sometimes taken, but there was something in the revolution wrought by Byrnes that looked like a concession to popular demand, and it was let go at that without being considered either very concernedly or very seriously. Mr. Byrnes had said that it was for the good of the Department, and Mr. Byrnes had organized the finest detective bureau in the known world ; therefore the public were easily contented to take his word for it.

At that time the blackmailing machinery of the Department was not as well understood by any of us as it is now, and there was one feature of the "Shake-Up" that could not, therefore, at that time, be appreciated, which is this, that when a new captain came into a "rich" precinct (rich in the sense of containing a goodly number of disorderly and gambling houses), a fresh levy is made on its gambling industries, presumably with the intent of indemnifying himself for the sum he has had to pay in order to secure the captaincy of such precinct; so that while a great shake-up looks like a strenuous effort on the part of the force to better its service, one of its most substantial effects is to stimulate certain of the shifting captains' revenue. The method by which this works was interestingly shown by Mrs. Schubert, in her testimony given before the Lexow Committee. Mrs. Schubert had been the keeper of a disorderly house on Chrystie Street, and we extract from her testimony as follows:

*Q.* How much money did you give up to Captain Cross?
*A.* Five hundred dollars.
*Q.* Where did you pay that money?
*A.* In my house.
*Q.* Did he go into the house for it?
*A.* Yes, sir.
*Q.* What did he say?
*A.* Just introduced himself, that he was the new captain and that he wanted five hundred dollars and fifty dollars every month.

. . . . . . . . .

*Q.* Was there anything said when you gave him the five hundred dollars about your being able to do business?
*A.* Well, yes; he said I would be protected, to run along quiet and not make any disturbance, fighting, or any noise; just to run my business quietly.

. . . . . . . . . .

*Q.* When Captain Cross went away Captain Devery came there did he not?
*A.* Yes.
*Q.* Did you have a visit from Captain Devery?
*A.* The same kind of a visit. He came to the house and introduced himself as a new captain.
*Q.* What did he say about money?
*A.* Well, five hundred dollars.

. . . . . . . . . .

*Q.* You were doing business before Captain Cross came into the precinct, weren't you?
*A.* McLaughlin was there.
*Q.* Did you have an interview with Captain McLaughlin?
*A.* The same thing.
*Q.* Did Captain McLaughlin demand money from you?
*A.* Yes, sir.
*Q.* What did he say?
*A.* Five hundred dollars.

. . . . . . . . . .

Those who are not familiar with the sort of testimony that was brought out by the Lexow Committee will be able to gain some notion of it from the above quotations. Our principal object in citing them, however, was to show the financial side of a "shake-up." A "shake-up" means, at least in the three cases just specified (and these are probably only a fair sample of most of the rest), that when Captain Jones is transferred to Captain Smith's precinct, and vice versa, Jones and Smith both are able to pocket five hundred dollars initiation fee from each of the disreputable houses in their new precincts respectively. "Shake-ups" look like police activity, but the most that they mean is a new twist on the extortion screw. It is a favorite expression used by Mr. Byrnes in connection with the transfer of captains, that it was done "for the good of the service." The above statement of Mrs. Schubert (which has been manifoldly corroborated) will give to the unsophisticated reader a new conception of what Mr. Byrnes means by "*the good of the service.*"

Such, then, is the estimate we have to form of the great police "Shake-up" of April 19th, when interpreted in the light of disclosures that have been since made. A repetition of that move would now be instantly resented as a shilly-shallying affectation on Mr. Byrnes's part, and an insult to the integrity and good sense of the town. As was distinctly disclosed by the testimony given by Commissioner Sheehan before the Lexow Committee, this shifting of the captains was carried out in accordance with a memorandum furnished by the Superintendent, which shows two things : First, the amount of subterfuge of which the Superintendent will avail when he is laboring for popular effect; second, the amount of power which he has been able to exercise notwithstanding his chronic pretence that he was practically restrained from all executive action by the embarrassing limitations put upon him by the Police Commissioners.

It would be a libel upon the Superintendent's insight

as police officer, to imagine that he thought that any permanent advantage would accrue to the city from a recast of the fields in which respectively a lot of criminals and incompetents should perform their office ; and it would be just as much of a libel upon Mr. Byrnes's sagacity, to suppose that he had not a clear comprehension of the criminal system of barter that obtained in the Department in the purchase of opportunities and the sale of immunities.

Mr. Byrnes has recently been reported in the *Tribune* of November, 1894, as saying that, in view of the disclosures made by the Lexow Committee, he thought the police force ought to be thoroughly reorganized. In other words, having been a member of the police force here for thirty-one years—patrolman, roundsman, sergeant, captain, inspector, superintendent—it took a committee, largely made up of gentlemen from outside of the city, to show this old police veteran the foul rottenness in the midst of which he had been for almost a third of a century wading and plying the officer ; and yet there are men in this city to-day urging that Mr. Byrnes shall help reorganize our police force.

We have been thus explicit in this part of our recital in order that it may be understood what some of the difficulties are against which the thorough and earnest sentiment of community has to contend in its efforts radically to improve our municipal condition. This was only one of a long series of instances in which the high police officials kept a careful finger on the general pulse, and made a showy demonstration of virtue when popular blood was approaching fever mark. The issue demonstrated, however, that there was no change in the spirit and purpose of the Department. Viewed with reference to the possibilities of blackmailing, there is pretty good soil over almost the whole of Manhattan Island, and a police captain who has been for any length of time on the force possesses a quick facility for sinking his roots anywhere ; and the process of being "shifted" works no substantial diminution of his revenue if, as he is likely to succeed in doing, he arranges to have his old trusted wardman graze for him in his new pasture.

## CHAPTER IX

### ON THE RACK

THE colossal piece of police posing which we have described under the title of "The Great Police Shake-up," produced its calculated effect, and the sentiment of community began immediately to rally to the support of the Department. The tide of popular indorsement that had been setting quite strongly in our favor since the presentment of March showed clear tokens of ebbing, and we could easily see that other influences, soon to be set in operation, would be almost certain to work in the same direction.

A number of indictments had been found by the March Grand Jury on the basis of evidence secured by Erving, Gardner, and myself, in the course of our tour of investigation. These cases must be tried and we must appear as witnesses. We have had a good many cases pigeon-holed, first and last, but we knew very well that these would not be.

So long as the results of our investigation of disorderly houses was stated only in the general terms employed in the discourse of March 13th, there was little likelihood that the public would take offence; but a jury trial does not stop with general statements, and the effect which Mr. Erving and myself easily anticipated as the issue, from the detailed canvass of the charges in question, would be to weaken the support of uncertain friends, and to arouse our enemies to a frenzy of affected loathing and hypocritical indignation. In neither of these respects were we disappointed. It was part of the plan of the campaign, however, and had to be gone through with. Those trials before the Court of General Sessions occurring early in May, marked a crisis in the history of the Reform Movement. We knew that if they were not conducted in such a way as to crush us, nothing could. No pains were spared to make us appear infamous. Practically it was not the keepers of disorderly resorts that were on trial, but Erving and myself. There is one public journal of whose conduct during those proceedings I cannot even to-day think without execrations that defy utterance. The loathsome malignity of the man whose genius inspired that sheet was just too human to be that of a beast, and a good deal too beastly to be that of a man. Time and event work their own revenges, however, and the rotten institution of which he was a part, and to which he ministered as a journalistic guardian angel, lies buried to-day beneath the ballots of a regenerated city.

I cannot fail, in this connection, to speak of the courteous, and even kindly treatment, which, during this ordeal, I experienced at the hands of Judge Fitzgerald; his single aim seemed to be to restrain the proceedings within the limits proper to a judicial investigation, and to correct the impression, assiduously cultivated, that it was the witness, not the defendant, that was on trial. To quote from the *World* of May 7th: "When the case (of Mrs. Adams) was begun, Lawyer Howe told the jury that he intended to show that Dr. Parkhurst was a criminal. As he uttered these words, Assistant District-Attorney McIntyre demanded that the Court protest against such language. Judge Fitzgerald asked that Mr. Howe confine himself to the limits of the case. 'The proper office of an opening address to the jury,' said the Judge, 'is to state the evidence that will be presented. The defendant is on trial, not Dr. Parkhurst.'"

Considering the character that has of late distinguished the District-Attorney's office of this city, and its confessed alliance with the system of maladministration against which we were battling, it might have been anticipated that the prosecuting officer in these cases would have discharged his office either traitorously or at least half-heartedly. On the contrary, too much cannot be said of the earnest faithfulness with which District-Attorney McIntyre threw himself into the work. As he remarked to me in a conference held somewhat later, when referring to these matters: "I made up my mind that the defendants were guilty and resolved to do my best to convict them."

It only remains to add that convictions followed in every case. Foreign as it has been to the purpose of the Society for the Prevention of Crime, during these three years past, to secure the punishment of individual criminals, yet the issue of the warrants just mentioned marked a certain amount of definite progress; it was a kind of judicial certificate to the fact that however mistaken we might be in our "methods," and however cranky we might be in our theories, when we said a thing was so, there was some likelihood at least that our statement was one that it was safe to tie to.

Notwithstanding the distinct language of criticism which we have just applied to one of our city dailies, we should be at fault if we did not, at the same time, recognize the valuable service it rendered to the cause, all undesignedly and unwittingly. Its viciousness was so vicious, and its malignity so malignant as to undo a good deal of its own work, defeat its own base ends, and initiate a reaction in our behalf. The American mind believes in fair play; and when the sheet referred to — the unconfessed organ of the unmentionable vices that were flourishing under Tammany patronage — had for some months dealt with Erving and myself and the Society for the Prevention of Crime as though we, and not the gamblers and the prostitutes and their police protectors, were the parties on trial, it began more and more to occur to our fellow-citizens that, while we might have been ex-

ceedingly injudicious in our methods, it was some
one besides ourselves that had been breaking the
laws, and that to hold us upon the editorial grid-
iron day after day, when the worst thing, perhaps, that
could be said of us was that we had undertaken in a
very questionable and injudicious way to ventilate the
official depravity for which the aforesaid journal stood
as sponsor, was not quite an ingenuous way of meeting the situation. This idea gained currency, and it
is to the conscienceless savagery of the editor of that
sheet, more than to any other one cause, I think, that
that growing currency was due.

It is to the influence above referred to that we were
indebted in part for the invitation that was extended
to us to discuss the question of "Christian Citizenship"
in Washington. A certain degree of remoteness enables one better to understand the conflict that is in
progress and to estimate the strength and quality of
the forces that are engaged. At any rate, the invitation came from Washington, and was significant for two
reasons; first, it was one indication that the contest
here in New York was coming to be interpreted as
something more than a local matter; and second,
emanating from the source it did, it was a testimonial
to the significance and dignity of the Reform Movement, and in that way worked encouragingly and contributed something toward turning the scale once
more in our favor.

The invitation to speak in Washington bore the

name of the Rev. Teunis S. Hamlin, pastor of the Church of the Covenant, in which the address was to be held, William Strong, H. L. Dawes, Charles C. Nott, John Wanamaker, and S. B. Elkins.

The meeting was presided over by President Rankin, of Howard University, who said, in the course of his remarks introducing the speaker :

"'The seed of the woman shall bruise the serpent's head.' This is the earliest prediction of the Messiah. This process is not agreeable to the serpent. Of course, he lifts his bruised head and gives vent to a great hiss, and all the little serpents hiss with him. It is the serpent's brood that has been disturbed. But notwithstanding all that, there is God's authority for the bruise.

"There is no sentimentality weaker than that which regards it right to condemn wicked things in preaching, but wrong to break them up in practice. There is no folly greater than to pay city officials to make laws and to enforce laws, and then to allow the same officials to connive at their violation ; to make common cause with the transgressors ; as the Bible expresses it, 'to consort with thieves and to be partakers with adulterers.'

"A man does not lay aside any of the prerogatives of citizenship by becoming a Christian minister ; he only consecrates them. Rev. Dr. Parkhurst, the distinguished citizen of New York, who has been invited to speak here by the pastor of this church, whose illness and family sorrow prevent his presence, well deserves the gratitude and honor here extended him. It is not exactly certain what the Apostle means when he says he fought with the wild beasts at Ephesus.

"What Dr. Parkhurst has done for New York he has not done for New York alone. He has done it for Washington and Chicago, and every other great city on this continent.

"If there is any shame in the act, we Christian citizens of this capital city of the nation wish by our presence here to participate in that shame. When a thing ought to be done, it must be done in the only manner in which it can be done. There is no inconsistency between the scourge of small cords for the back of the tempter, and the tender words, 'Neither do I condemn thee,' for the ear of the broken-hearted penitent. The Lion of the tribe of Judah is the Lamb of God that takes away the sin of the world."

Another symptom of the returning support of community, especially among the young men, was indicated by the gathering held at Scottish Rite Hall, on Madison Avenue, on the evening of May 12th, at which there were represented forty religious and secular societies of the city. It seemed as though the time had come for commencing to organize the earnest sentiment of the town into action. Conservative Christians and radical sinners were still propounding to themselves the question whether the whole movement was not a vicious one *ab initio*, and whether what they were inclined to think the criminality of my proceedings, did not acquit reputable people from all obligation to interfere with the evident criminality of the police in their proceedings. There were conferences enough held on the matter, and homiletical fireworks enough set off to inaugurate a new Lutheran Reformation, but in the meantime community was still standing with its arms akimbo, the police fostering and permitting crime after the same old diabolical way, and the town settling down more and more deeply into the quagmire of pecuniarily protected vice. There was, however, a large element of young life throughout the town that was willing to leave questions of casuistry to Howe & Hummel, Shechan, and an indeterminate clergy, and set its hands to the work of doing something to put a period to our municipal woe and dishonor. Hence the meeting in Scottish Rite Hall, May 12th. There were about seven hundred young men present from all parts of the city; they were not clear what they could do, but were confident that they could do something. The meeting was held under the auspices of the Society for the Prevention of Crime, several of whose directors were present, among others Louis L. Delafield, who presided, Chancellor MacCracken, Dr. J. N. Hallock, David J. Whitney, Frank Moss, E. A. Newell, and W. C. Stuart.

The following words, spoken by myself at that

time, are introduced here mainly for the significance that is given to them by the events that have transpired later :

"The fault with you and with me is that we do not individually recognize our own civic obligations to the city of which we are residents. In one sense of the term I have a profound admiration for Tammany Hall. It is an unquestioned fact that Tammany has richly earned the position of influence and of administrative power which she holds. She has been faithful, she has studied her own interests, she has looked to what she chooses to call her obligations, and by virtue of her fidelity she never takes a recess; she never goes off on a vacation, and through this devotion to herself she is what she is. There is a lesson in that. You can learn lessons even from the devil, in the point of fidelity and unswerving devotion to the one object that is in view. That same kind of fidelity, of constant and conscientious recognition of the relations in which we stand to our city, you and I have not exercised, and that explains our present situation. We have no right to sublet our obligations and let some one else exercise them in our behalf.

"Last night there was another raid in the Tenderloin gambling district. There is a good deal that is funny about these gambling-house raids. There were eighteen warrants secured by Mr. Byrnes. You have read in the Scriptures about the house that was empty, swept, and garnished. There is nothing so clean as a gambling-house before a raid. Among them was a warrant against Daly's gambling-house. These eighteen houses were raided, fourteen of them were clean and in the other four there was nothing going on, but some of the furniture was taken. There was a gentleman in my house last evening while this was going on. He had been out gambling. He said that he went up to Daly's. They told him, 'We would like to take you in but we are doing nothing now.' I could have told Mr. Byrnes myself that Daly's was not running. Well, they told this gentleman, 'We know you well, but we received instructions from the authorities to keep very close until the storm blows over.' Now, what kind of a municipal administration do you call that? Standing right in with each other. 'But,' says the darkey who had his eye in the slot of the door, 'I'll tell you what you can do. There is a place where, until the storm blows over, we are sending our patrons.' He went there, and, fortunately for him, he lost what little he had; and a singular thing about it is that that gambling-house, though situated in the same district, was not touched at all last night. Now this is hypocrisy; it is a lie straight through.

"We who are evangelical believe in a man's being born again. The city of New York administratively has got to be thoroughly born again. No slight modifications of policy that may be made, like the sending of a police captain from the Fourth Precinct to Goatville, or the sending of one from Goatville to the Fourth Precinct, will suffice. That does not touch the genius of the institution. It is thoroughly, inherently, and intrinsically corrupt, and it is bound to remain corrupt until the devil of Tammany Hall has been thoroughly cast out and the spirit of purity and honesty and administrative integrity has entered in its stead."

It was from this meeting that there developed the organization now known as the City Vigilance League. About two hundred of those present expressed a wish to enroll themselves for active service in the cause of municipal reform, and subscribed their names to pledge-cards which read as follows :

" I hereby pledge myself to study the municipal interests of this city, and to do everything in my power to promote the purity and honesty of its government."

A committee of five was designated to perfect an organization and to arrange for carrying forward work upon lines that had been laid down by the speakers of the evening. This committee consisted of A. S. Lyman, W. B. Young, H. K. Twitchell, R. M. Lloyd, and C. H. Parkhurst, and its plan of action was submitted and adopted on the 18th of the same month.

It would be off from the main line of our purpose to enter into the details of the organization and work of the City Vigilance League ; it will suffice to say that it embraces the entire city in its scheme of operation. Local organizations have been established in each of the thirty Assembly Districts of the city, and the leaders of those districts respectively compose the central committee upon which devolves the responsibility of the entire organization. Each Assembly District leader associates with himself trusty men, sufficient in number to have each election district represented, requiring in all, therefore, 1,141 workers, with such additional number, however, as the exigencies of the case in the special election district may require. This enables the League to keep in touch with each specific locality throughout the entire town.

The League is mortgaged to no sect and to no school of politics ; its members are not seeking office, and we are bound by the terms of our constitution to put forward no candidates for office. Our aim is to acquaint ourselves with our city, to study its needs, to publish existing abuses whatever may be the party or whoever may be the man that may be responsible for them, and to stimulate, especially among the young men, both of our native and foreign population, that understanding of municipal interests that shall help to make the municipal ballot intelligent, and that appreciation of civic duties that shall help to render the municipal ballot clean and honest. In a word, the League represents the continuance of that straight line of rectitude and individual self-regardlessness needed in order to win the victory of November, and just as much needed in order to render the fruits of that victory an abiding possession.

# CHAPTER X

### MASS MEETING AT COOPER UNION

As soon as it was generally known that the Society for the Prevention of Crime was unreservedly committed to the public interest and that it was making war on crime, and in particular on the police as the salaried protectors of crime, lines of confidence and of intercommunication began presently to open themselves between such as were being offended or injured by the existing lawlessness, and our Society, so that we were soon able to know, with great accuracy, the condition of affairs in every part of the city. Out of some thousands of such letters received during the last two or three years, we reproduce here the following as fair samples, premising that the first inserted was addressed to Dr. Howard Crosby and written as long ago as 1879, when Captain (now Superintendent) Byrnes ("Burns") was in charge of the precinct to which "Broken-hearted wife's" complaint refers. It is at least fifteen years, therefore, since Byrnes began to become acquainted with the iniquitous system here prevailing, and which he has lacked the moral courage to expose.

NEW YORK CITY, July 29, 1879.

REV. HOWARD CROSBY.

SIR: If you will break up the gambling hells in Bleecker Street, Thompson, and the low dance houses or stores turned into halls, you will do the Christian community a service, and save many a poor woman who is on the road to ruin. I have seen mothers begging their children home from these places night after night. Captain Burns of the Police says he can't break them up as they have political influence behind them. See if you cannot.

    (Signed)  A HEART-BROKEN WIFE.

KIND SIR: I would like you to close a policy shop. It has been running for a long time. I am a citizen of this country and I do not think it is right to have them things in this country or in this city. I have wrote to Police Headquarters and it did no good, so I thought I would write to you and see if you would be so kind as to close it up. You would receive the thanks of me and many a sufferer of the game. It is located at a cigar store, — Washington Street, New York City.

        Yours truly,
  (Signed)  A TRUE CITIZEN OF THIS COUNTRY.

NEW YORK, December 26, 1894.

REV. CHAS. E. PARKHURST.

DEAR SIR: I read the *World* every day, and like very much the way you show up the police. I know a policy-shop here that pays $25.00 per month for protection (the writer tells me himself), and I have seen him write as high as $30.00 per day, and seen children as young as ten years, yes eight years, bring in plays, and I know he has been arrested a couple of times and is out on bond. He gets $2.50 a day when arrested.

He says if there is anything in the wind the Central lets him know in time.

I could write and tell you more if I was sure I would not be known, or would not get my name in the newspapers. I know this shop is a rank swindle, and could easily be broken up if the detectives wanted to.

I hope you will not let any reporter get a copy of this, for if the writer (policy) should see it he might suspect. I was coming to see you at your residence, but was not sure I would be able to see you. If I could show up this place without being known, I would.                    Yours truly,
            (Signed)    JOSEPH BROWN.

NOTE.—Of course the above is not my true name, but will do.                                      J. B.

                            December 12, 1894.

DEAR DOCTOR: Won't you *please* try and close the policy-shop at —— Seventh Avenue, between Thirty-first and Thirty-second Streets. The people all go in through the cigar store next door. He has a private door in the back of his store. The policy-shop is the biggest one in the whole district. The police know all about it, but don't care. *Please*, Dr. Parkhurst, close this infamous and dirty hole. The saloon at ——, next door, is just as bad.

            (Signed)    MOTHER WITH FOUR BOYS.

NEW YORK, December 24, 1894.
REV. DR. CHAS. H. PARKHURST,
　No. 133 East Thirty-fifth Street,
　　　New York City.

DEAR SIR: After repeated notices to the police to remedy the following evil, with no attention paid to them at all, I call upon you, as a last resource, and, I think, a sure one.

There is a liquor store at No. —— Rivington Street which is, in reality, a gambling hell of the worst character. It is open all night and on Sunday is open all day, and inhabited by at least one hundred persons who lose all their wages and worse.

The owner admits that he pays police protection, and the officer on the post goes in there for his daily glass of beer.

If you can do anything to close this one of many evil places, you will confer a great favor on,
　　　　Yours respectfully,
　　　　　　(Signed)　　　　——.

Such correspondence has been an invaluable aid to us. A very large proportion of the letters that have come to hand were anonymous, and therefore of no value as before a court of law; but they were of unspeakable assistance to us as indicating the lines upon which we could most confidently work, and by their aid, supplemented by that of our detectives, we have been able to know from one day to another, just what was transpiring throughout the city, what orders were being given from station-houses or from headquarters, and have known with what degree of rigor or laxity laws were being enforced in the several precincts.

We soon discovered that a sudden enforcement of law was but a desire to hoodwink the public, and that a raid was a contrivance by which the Superintendent, or his subordinates, attempted to amuse themselves and delude a credulous community. It took us some months to learn that a raid was not to be taken seriously. If there are two notorious gambling-houses or disorderly houses side by side, and one of them is raided and the other not, only a fool will imagine that there was any more honesty in raiding one of the two than in leaving the other unraided. That course of procedure has obtained in this city for three years, and obtains to-day. Notwithstanding all this spasmodic activity that prevailed during the months of April and May, the Society for the Prevention of Crime knew, and to some extent the people of the town suspected that there was no change of sentiment or of intention on the part of the Police Department, and if there were to be any improved municipal condition it would have to come from a grand forward movement and a concerted protest on the part of the people at large.

All of this paved the way for the Cooper Union Hall Mass Meeting of May 26th. There had been a rising demand for such meeting for some weeks. The *Mail and Express* had, for a long time been engaged in fearless warfare against police corruption, and in its issue of May 13th (the date following the meeting at Scottish Rite Hall), printed the following under the caption :

"NOW FOR A MEETING."

More than two hundred young men, enthusiastic, intelligent, and profoundly in earnest, agreed last night, at the close of Dr. Parkhurst's address at Scottish Rite Hall, to stand by him in his noble work. This is the kind of Americanism and patriotism that the hour and emergency demand. The work will grow and the workers will increase from day to day.

It is the old story. The combat against sin is always with the right. The people are slow to move, but when their eyes are opened to the gravity of the situation, when the battle begins, battalion follows battalion in the service of conscience until the overthrow of the enemy becomes complete annihilation.

There never was another such opportunity for a reform movement in this city. The iniquities of Tweed pale into insignificance beside the blackmailing operations on a stupendous scale of this Tammany-ridden city. Dr. Parkhurst has only lifted a corner of the blanket. If half of the truth were known the world would stand aghast at the frightful revelation.

Think of the administration of the greatest city in the United States, and one of the greatest in the world, being in league with criminals, challenged with the proof of the fact, convicted of the crime and yet defying public opinion, as Tammany defies it to-day.

The Society for the Prevention of Crime was disposed to withhold its support and encouragement of such a meeting, doubting whether the time were yet quite ripe for it, and fearing that its effect would be to draw more sharply the line of demarcation between those who sympathized with us and those who did not. The pressure, however, became stronger than could easily be resisted ; the call was issued and the meeting held. This was on the 27th of May. David J. Whitney and Dr. J. N. Hallock were the ones most active in perfecting the arrangements. The Society for the Prevention of Crime has always been most loyal to the memory of its first president, Dr. Howard Crosby, and his portrait hung back of the stage. The hall was crowded to its utmost capacity, the audience containing a fair percentage of women. Dr. Hallock called the meeting to order and ex-Judge Arnoux was made Chairman.

The Chairman outlined the history of the movement and set forth its purposes. " Many present," he said, " are laboring under the misapprehension that this crusade is aimed against specific houses of a criminal character. Its guns, however, are levelled at higher aims. The object of the movement is to make the police do their duty, and their whole duty, or stand before the world convicted of the presentment of the March Grand Jury."

Ex-Judge Noah Davis, whose participation in the breaking of the Tweed Ring made his interest in the present cause both so natural and so gratifying, was then introduced and enthusiastically greeted. He began by saying that the present demonstration reminded him of the uprising of the people twenty years before, and enlarged upon the part which at that time had been played in the Tweed overthrow by Samuel J. Tilden and Charles O'Conor. He continued: "You have come here to answer the question whether or not your boys shall be brought up in the midst of officially protected crime. If you say that that shall not be done, you can only say it just now by your applause, but later, by your hearty devotion to those who have courage to pluck aside the curtain and show just where we live, and what we are, and what is around us. Most men tell us that the President of this Society should never have done what he has done; that a minister of the Gospel should spend his whole life persuading mankind to make some atonement for the sin of Adam; that he should let all modern Adams alone; that he should preach upon the old line, 'In Adam's fall we sinned all.' I make no pretensions to fighting Adam myself, but if I had been brought face to face with the situation that confronted Dr. Parkhurst, if my charges had been denied, if a District-Attorney had laughed at me, if a Grand Jury had pointed the finger of scorn at me, I would have dived to the bottom of hell, if need be, to prove that I had spoken the truth. If there be clergymen in this country, or this city, or anywhere, who say they could not have gone through such a thing, all I have to say is that they know more about themselves than I know. By that I mean only just what you think I mean."

Rabbi F. De Sola Mendes spoke in part, as follows:
"I presume that the privilege accorded me of speaking a few earnest words at a notable gathering like this, and on an occasion so auspicious of excellent result for the city in which we are proud to dwell, must be owing to the fact that I am a member, albeit one of the least important, of a Society for the Suppression of Crime, which boasts of a very rare antiquity. It is a Society older than this of New York, older than Manhattan even, older than the United States, older than the mother-country, England; in fact, just as old as the Jewish nation. When Almighty God, in the infinitude of His wisdom, selected a certain family of the families of the earth to evangelize the crying iniquity, the foul vice and sin of what is conveniently called Canaanite 'Idolatry,' then the first Society for the Suppression of Vice was formed, and Israel was its name. Though many another and many a better expounder of that Society's fundamental maxim, 'Holy shall ye be, for holy am I, the Lord your God,' could have been found to speak to you to-night, it is because that divine commission touches and imbues even the least of His servants that I, in behalf of your Hebrew fellow-citizens, have come to cry 'God speed' to the good work so unexpectedly, so significantly, and I may say so triumphantly, put on foot of late. . . .

"You have said, Dr. Parkhurst, that it was at the funeral of our departed friend, who is up there, Rev. Dr. Howard Crosby of blessed memory, that you took upon yourself the vow to continue his work. I, too, heard the hearty tribute paid that day to the illustrious dead, and can imagine the surge of noble emotion which came to you then. He was the Moses: be you the Joshua. And as I take my seat, let me repeat to you the olden words we have cherished among us, spoken to Joshua by our Almighty Father in a similar emergency in our leader's life, when he, too, was thrust to the front by God's call to war upon and stamp out the immorality and vice in Canaan : 'There shall not any man be able to stand before thee all the days of thy life; as I was with Moses so I will be with thee; I will not fail thee, I will not forsake thee. Only be strong and very courageous to observe to do according to all the law which Moses my servant commanded thee; turn not to the right hand nor to the left, that thou mayest have good success whithersoever thou goest. Have I not commanded thee? Be strong and of good courage; be not afraid, neither be thou dismayed, for the Lord thy God is with thee whithersoever thou goest.' Amen."

Following Rabbi Mendes, Rev. Dr. David J. Burrell, after having spoken of Superintendent Byrnes in terms of commendation, went on to say :

"There is a reservation in Superintendent Byrnes's recent letter which I do not like. He does not seem to be in full sympathy with the law. He seems to be enforcing the law because he is obliged to do it, not because he is in sympathy with it. He tells us that the best way to deal with the brothels would be to localize them and put them under the surveillance of the police force. We have not appointed Superintendent Byrnes, who is but the servant of the people, to tell us what laws there ought to be. It is not his function to legislate; it is not his function even to moralize to the people; we ministers can do most of the moralizing, and what we do not do you can do after us; but the only man in this town who has not any right to moralize is the Superintendent of the Police; he is appointed just to keep quiet and do what the people tell him to do. What we demand—I like that word 'demand'—what we, the sovereign people, demand, is that the law shall be enforced. The people are in this thing, and we mean business."

Frank Moss, Esq., counsel of the Society for the Prevention of Crime was then introduced, and although speaking briefly, handled with the wisdom begotten of intimate acquaintance, the matter of the Police Commissioners and the little confidence that could be reposed in them as a tribunal for the trial of captains. He said in part:

"Since I began to observe these matters, four police captains have been tried on charges of tolerating vice. The result of each trial was a tie vote—two Commissioners voting the captain guilty and two not guilty. I was present at three of the trials. In the first the evidence was overwhelming that vice of the worst kind had been tolerated for years on the same block with the station-house, notwithstanding complaints of citizens, the houses being regularly reported by the captain as disorderly.

"The tie vote of the Board has never been altered, but, curiously, one of the Commissioners who voted the captain guilty, at the same session voted to promote him in order to break a dead-lock, as he said. In the two cases next tried, the gambling-houses which had long been reported by captains at headquarters, were raided at the instance of private persons, without the knowledge or co-operation of the captains, and the gamblers were convicted. The captains were charged with neglect of duty. Two Commissioners voted them guilty and two not guilty."

A series of resolutions was presented and adopted as follows :

We, citizens of New York, assembled at Cooper Union Hall, May 26, 1892, at the invitation of the Society for the Prevention of Crime, to consider the subject of crime and its official toleration, do adopt the following resolutions :

1. We cordially thank the Rev. Charles H. Parkhurst, President of the Society for the Prevention of Crime, for his courageous and self-sacrificing stand in calling public attention to protected crime, and for his patriotic endeavor to enlist our citizens in the work of purifying their own city ; and we pledge our sympathy and support to him and to that Society in the great work which they have undertaken. We recog-

nize in Dr. Parkhurst qualities of heroism and persistency which endear him to us.

2. We thank the Grand Jury of March, 1892, for the promptness and fidelity with which it investigated the subject as presented by Dr. Parkhurst for the Society, and for its now famous presentment.

3. We demand the prompt enforcement by the District-Attorney, and the Police Department, and by all other departments and officials of our government, of all laws for the prevention of vice.

4. We invoke such action by those who are thereto empowered as will destroy the present system of official toleration and protection of vice and crime, and will bring to speedy justice such officials particularly as fail to discharge their duties because of complicity with evil-doers.

5. We demand prompt and vigorous procedure by the District-Attorney and others who have authority against all property-owners and agents who let houses for illegal purposes. (Long applause.) Let the axe fall on those who reap golden harvests from vice, whether they be officials, real-estate owners, or agents.

6. We demand that the Police Department proceed at once and vigorously against the proprietors and owners of gambling and disorderly houses as required by Sections 282 and 285 of the Consolidation Act.

7. For the present condition of protected crime we hold responsible, not only the owners of property and police officials, but also those men and newspapers who make common cause with criminals. Most especially we hold responsible those men who are in political control of our government, and who could the most speedily grant the reforms that are so greatly

needed. We pledge to each other our best efforts to compel those in authority to honestly and earnestly enforce the criminal laws.

I shall be excused for adding the closing paragraph from my own address, expressing, as that paragraph does, the spirit with which the Society for the Prevention of Crime has been steadily animated through all its hard warfare :

"This is a long movement. We are not working for next November. There is nothing that a live old or young man will find worth working for that does not reach away into the future. Let us not be discouraged. Defeats are sometimes the very material of victory. I do profoundly thank the February Grand Jury for the defeat which it dealt out to me. If it had not been for De Lancey Nicoll and the February Grand Jury, I should not have been here to-night. It takes sometimes a quick lash to stir up the serious part of our nature.

"Though the battle be a long one we all believe, in our consciences and before God, that victory is in front of us, and victory for New York means victory for every large city in the country, and when you have redeemed the cities of the country, you have redeemed the country in its entirety.

"If one had known nothing of the criminal strength of the Police Department or of the depth to which its roots had thrust themselves into the slimy, oozy soil of Tammany Hall, it would have seemed as though on the evening of the 26th of May, 1892, little remained but to enjoy the fruits of the victory already gained ; or, if one had taken the gathering in Cooper Union Hall that evening as a fair expression of the convictions of the city at large, even in its better elements, the conclusion would have been instantaneous that popular sentiment was already ripe for the overthrow of a municipal system against which the oratory at that mass meeting was so steadily directed, and against which the sentiment of that enthusiastic audience was so unequivocally expressed. The fact was, however, that the feeling of the police toward us at that time was not at all one of fear, but only of irritation, and that the great mass of our population regarded the movement far more with interested curiosity than it did with heated earnestness. The public sensation incident to the Cooper Union meeting did not yet issue from that point in men's hearts at which they keep their solid determinations and their moral indignation. Perhaps we did not realize it at that time, but the lesson was learned toilsomely and painfully in the eighteen months following.

## CHAPTER XI

### THE PULPIT AND POLITICS

THERE has been, during the past three years, a good deal of discussion as to the relation proper to exist between the pulpit and municipal politics. I have had no disposition to crowd my own views of that matter upon others' acceptance. Having reached a conviction of my own, I acted accordingly; and while recognizing that others have as much right to their opinion as I to mine, it has sometimes seemed as though, if, instead of spending so much time in publishing and fortifying their opinion, they had dropped argumentation and gone to work to minister to the city in some better way of their own, it would have saved a great deal of unnecessary rhetoric and accomplished more toward recovering us from our municipal dishonor.

While, however, I had no wish to force my opinions upon others, I was very willing to express them to any that were desirous of hearing them, and accordingly, at the request of the Alumni of the Union Theological Seminary, in this city, prepared the following address (which seems to me not out of place in a record of this kind), and which was delivered at the Seminary Building on the 14th of May, 1894, as follows :

I am to speak of the relation of the minister to good government. In order to avoid all misapprehension, let us start out by saying that nothing should be allowed to interfere with the pulpit's prime obligation to convert men, women, and children to Christ in their individual character. No one can have attended carefully to Christ's method of working in the world without appreciating the emphasis which he laid upon the *individual*, and without feeling the volume of meaning there is in the fact that so many of his finest words and deepest lessons were delivered in the presence of but a single auditor. There are no associate results which do not hide all their roots in the separate individualities that combine to compose such association.

At the same time, what God thinks most of is not a man in his individual character, but men in their mutual and organized relations. That is the idea that the Bible leaves off upon, and in that way throws upon the idea the superb emphasis of finality, culminating, as Scripture does, not in the roll-call of a mob of sanctified individualities, but in the apocalyptic forecast of a *holy city* come down from God out of heaven ; not men, therefore, taken as so many separate integers, but men conceived of as wrought up into the structure of a corporate whole—social, municipal, civic.

Men require to be sanctified, but the relations which subsist between them require to be sanctified also. Philemon was a Christian and Onesimus was a Christian; but Onesimus was still Philemon's slave. Philemon had been converted, and Onesimus had been converted, but the *relation* between them had not been converted. A good part of every man is involved in his relations, and heaven is not arithmetic but organic.

Wherever men rub against one another, therefore, the pulpit has something to say, or ought to have something to say. This enhances prodigiously the opportunities and obligations of the pulpit, and ought to affect and modify very seriously the preparation wherewith a young man equips himself for pulpit service. It is simply appalling, the area of inquiry which at once opens itself before him and challenges his regard so soon as he realizes that the consummation of his mission is not to save from hell as many separate people as he can, but to become, in God's hands, the means of saving society here and now, and precipitating heaven by constructing as much terrestrial heaven as possible out of materials already in hand. That is an idea that is working in the current mind, and that our theological seminaries are beginning to evince symptoms of regard for. It is a conception of the case that is well-nigh staggering so soon as you begin to realize how little of a man's practical life is an individual affair, and what a vast percentage of it concerns him in his relations to his fellows.

You may take a very large percentage of the great questions that are always under discussion—social questions and political questions—and you will discover that such questions are nothing more nor less than crystallizations about an ethical nucleus. They are not altogether ethical, but they revolve on an ethical axis, and the pulpit wants to be prepared to manipulate such questions with a firm hand, rend the ethical elements from such as are morally indifferent, and then take the ethical elements in their clear separateness and exhibit them, by which I mean *preach them*. There is not a live question in society or in State to-day that is not nine-tenths of it a question of morals. And before the pulpit handles it it has got to know how much of it lies within ethical ground and how much without ; for woe be to the preacher who undertakes to deal homiletically with such aspects of a question as are relevant not to the pulpit but to the expert.

All of this work means straining solidity of preparation. It is worse than Greek, tougher than Hebrew, or than almost any of the other antiques that ordinarily ornament the curriculum of a theological seminary. Undoubtedly the handling of these matters in the pulpit means friction. But there will always be friction when there is power on its way to effect, so that need not alarm anybody. History is going up hill, not down, and that always means heated bearings and squeak in the wheels.

Of course there is a way of preaching that will keep the axles cool. Unquestionably we might expatiate eloquently on historic unrighteousness, and the greater the eloquence the greater the favor with which we should be followed. We can malign David for his vices, and pour canister-shot into poor Solomon for his irregularities; and his being a back number and having no extant relatives to pound you with a libel suit, the whole performance reduces to an elegant sedative, just warm enough to stimulate the blood if the church is cold, and cold enough to discourage perspiration if it is July.

Here are certain moral ideas to be pushed. Who is going to push them if the pulpit does not? Here are certain breaches of moral propriety and decency on the part of the national or the municipal government. Who is going to protest, if the pulpit does not? Do you say that that is going outside of your diocese? Well, what is your diocese? Are you one of God's prophets, visioned with an eye that sees right and wrong with something of the distinctness of divine intuition, and are you going to let that wrong lie there as so much ethical rot and close your eyes to it and pray, "Thy kingdom come?"

That was the superb feature of the old prophets of the Hebrews: they were statesmen; they so grasped the times in their living and pregnant realities that everything stood out before their inspired and burning thought in solid relation to the Kingdom of God. There was no splitting up of things into holy and civic. That splitting and slicing process is one of the old serpent's shrewdest devices for getting the biggest half of the world in the range of his own quivering fangs. Those old prophets of the Hebrews were statesmen. They could not help being. Their eye went so deep and wide that of necessity they flung their arm about everything. There is not a great deal of statesmanship in the pulpit to-day, and outside of it there is not any—that I know of. There is politics, but there is not statesmanship. Do you know what the difference is between statesmanship and politics? Well, politics is statesmanship with the moral gristle left out. Politics in certain respects is a good deal worse than depravity, pure and simple. Thoroughbred depravity has the courage of its viciousness. About politics there is just that tincture of decency that makes it unreliable. I have had to deal with men that were elaborately and consistently wicked, and I have had to deal with politicians, and I would rather cope with ten of the former than one of the latter. The politician is like one of those agile and cheerful little beasts which, if you put your hand where he isn't, he's there; and put your hand where he is, and he isn't there.

So I say, where are you going to get your statesmanship unless you get it from the prophets and the pulpits? It used to abound at Washington. How long has it been since anybody at Washington has stood up in the strength of a Wilson, a Sumner, a Webster, or an Elijah, and spoken the word that has drawn to a snugger tension the moral sense of this great people? We used to have speeches made there that would ring clear across the continent, and clear the air for a decade. There are themes enough to talk about now, and there are brains enough to talk about them, but it takes something besides brains to lift to a higher tone the national conscience, and to stimulate to a quicker and fuller pulse the national life. There is not the Samson at Washington that will fling his arms about the two pillars and bow himself mightily, for while he might like to shake off the Philistines on the roof, he fears more the inconvenience of being dusted by the *débris* and crushed on the underside of the collapse. We never feel quite so confident of the perpetuity of American institutions as we do just after Congress has adjourned, and Senators and Representatives have packed their gripsacks and gone home. We feel about Congress in our civic relations very much as most of us here to-day do about General Assembly in our ecclesiastical relations, —we wish that it were at least four years between sessions: in fact the longer the better.

And I am afraid we shall not be much better rewarded for our quest if we search for statesmanship in the files of the newspaper press. This is not denying the braininess of the press, nor its power, nor the immense value of the service which it renders along specific lines. But when you come to consider the secular press as a *moral* force, it is not there. I do not mean that there is no paper published, no paper in this city published, that is a quickener of the moral energies of this city and community. What I mean is that the daily press is, with hardly an exception, run by its business end. The editorial page is definitely determined by monetary considerations. Journals are not printed for the sake of stating and pushing the truth. No man can ever do a thoroughly good thing when he is primarily motived thereto by the dollar. You cannot preach an inspiring sermon when you feel the money there is in it, nor any more can you fill a column with editorial electricity when you feel the money there is in it. The more a paper puts in the pockets of its stockholders, the less, probably, it puts into the hearts and lives of its readers. Under existing conditions, then, you cannot with much confidence look to the newspapers for statesmanship, for statesmanship has got to have an ethical element, and ethics doesn't pay. If you go into ethic business, you will have to dispense with terrapin or live on a legacy.

So that at present if you are going to have statesmen you will have to look to the pulpit for them. And there is not a better place for them. There is no place where one would have any better right to expect them to abound. Ninety per cent. of the material of social and civic questions being ethical, what reason is there why pulpit prophets should not marshal the army of event? They used to do so, why shouldn't they now? If there is any Moses who can climb onto the top of Sinai and commune with God and behold with an unabashed eye the realities that compose the tissue of all history, why should he not lead the waiting host when he gets back to the foot of the mountain? Why leave it to dirty Aaron, who meantime has been stripping the people and building golden calves?

I am not talking about holding the offices! To the evil one with your offices! I am talking about holding the sceptre over the consciences of people and swinging them into beat with the pulse of the heart of God, and into pace with the trend of his eternal purpose. That is the only governance we have any care for, and it is the only governance that governs too. Talk about the diminishing power of the pulpit? There is power enough if the pulpit will rise to the stature of its prophetic dignity, and assert itself and exercise its power. I do not believe that so far forth the pulpit was ever so powerful as it is to-day. I do do not believe that virtue ever respected it more, or that vice ever hated it and feared it more than it does to-day. If the pulpit is honest, intelligent, untrammelled, anxious for nothing so much as to be the oracle of God and to see the Lord's Prayer turned into history, why, there is nothing that can stand alongside of it in point of conscious and confident authority. It seizes questions on those sides that are correlated with the conscience, and handles them with that poise of assurance and challenge that stirs up no end of malignity perhaps, but that allows no room for retreat; handles them, too, with that long regard and with that impassioned sense of whatsoever is eternal that obviates the necessity of partisan discount. There is not a knave in this city, nor any corporation of knaves, that would not rather have its character portrayed by the most influential journal in town, than to have it portrayed by a Christian minister; always being understood though by a Christian minister, one who tells the truth as before God and only for the truth's sake, and who is prepared to keep telling it till he wears through the epidermis into the quick.

When you know you are right, and can feel it all through you, just as distinctly as Elijah, standing up in front of Ahab, felt the three years' drought that was coming, there is a dash of omnipotence in the word you speak. Its censures fall upon current iniquity with the hard thud of a sledge-hammer. The possibilities of all statesmanship are in it, for it beholds as with prophetic vision, the thread of eternal principle upon which alone the events of history can be permanently strung; and so is qualified, as with the incisiveness and fearlessness of prophetic utterance, to state eternal principle in a manner to the bracing of virtue and the paralysis of vice.

And I am saying what I know. I uttered only thirty minutes of indictment against the blood-sucking scoundrels that are draining the veins of our body municipal, and they were all set wriggling like a lot of muck-worms in a hot shovel. I am not such a fool as to suppose that it was the man that said it that did the work ; nor that it was what was said that did the work, for it had been said a hundred times before with more of thoroughness and detail.

*It was the pulpit that did the work.* Journalistic roasting these vagabonds will enjoy and grow cool over. But when it is clear that the man who speaks it is speaking it not for the purpose of putting money into his pocket or power into his party, but is speaking it because it is true, and in speaking it appreciates his oracular authority as one commissioned of God to speak it, there is a suggestion of the Judgment-Day about it, there is a presentiment of the invisible God back of it, that knots the stringy conscience of these fellows into contortions of terror. Waning power of the pulpit? There is all of power in the pulpit that there is of God voicing Himself through the man who stands in the pulpit.

Now, my brethren in the Christian ministry, here is a field for you ; a field that is as broad as your intelligence, and as vast as the indwelling Spirit with which you have been divinely baptized. It is *your* field. If your ministry is being rendered in this city, for instance, the associate life of this city, with all of civic concern that goes to make up that life, is as justly subject to the mastery of your inspired and imperial words as were the people of Israel amenable to the holy dictatorship of a Moses, a Samuel, an Elijah. Do not allow yourselves to be ostracized from your own kingdom and your own throne either by custom, cowardice, or the devil. I know we are told that we ought not to mix in the earthy pursuits or to trail our clerical robes through the dust of this secular life ! The idea of a rabble of cut-throats, thieves, thugs and libertines presuming to stand up and tell God's prophets to keep their hands off of the ark of the covenant when the sole regard they have for the ark is their sacrilegious appetite for the golden pot of manna that is preserved in the interior of the ark ! Don't let these dirty hypocrites fool you. There is moral material enough in community but it lacks leadership. The prophets of God are here to meet that exigency. That is what they are for ; to foster and train moral sentiment, to compact and marshal it, and hold it along lines of earnest and intelligent devotement to the common weal.

This does not at all involve entrance into the details of matters and becoming personally complicated in the intricacies of administration. That is another affair altogether, and one for which the prophet's previous training can scarcely be supposed to make him competent. But the determinative factor in all personal government (as opposed to brute government) is a matter of moral sentiment, and that is a commodity of which God's pulpit servants are, *ex officio*, the priests.

There are all sorts of influences — the influence of pelf, the influence of self-seeking, the influence of partisanship — which is simply self-seeking on an enlarged scale — there are all sorts of influences that are operating powerfully to degrade the quality of associate life, and to debase the tone of civic administration, and the pulpit is the source to which you have got to look for that counteracting energy which shall set truth and righteousness before the people in that substantiality of body and definedness of outline which shall quicken the thought, impress the conscience, invigorate the purpose, nerve the arm, and drive sneaking iniquity to cover. Try to conceive what would be the effect upon this city if but a dozen of the representative prophets of each of the denominations were to conceive of themselves, severally, as standing before the collective and impersonated depravity of our municipality in the same attitude of conscious divine authority in which Elijah confronted Ahab; by next November you would not have enough Tammany Hall left to make it real interesting to depict it.

My brethren in the Ministry, if I have spoken earnestly I have spoken so because I feel the situation and know that not a word has been uttered but what is as true as holy writ. Our national security, the achievement of what we believe to be our national destiny is not a matter of wealth nor of population, nor of territorial area, it is a matter of national righteousness; it is a matter of honest laws honestly executed. It is a matter of nominating to positions of official responsibility, and electing when they have been nominated, and sustaining when they have been elected, men who are God-fearing, who respect truth because it is true, righteousness because it is holy, and who conceive of office as a sacred trust, and a holy stewardship. Now, brother, to take an overt and aggressive position in pursuance of that end, eulogizing official integrity and damning official corruption, is part of the duty to which you are called. There is no man that can do it or that can begin to do it with so much effect as an accredited and anointed prophet of God. Men do not care for men, but words that betray the symptoms of a divine sanction fasten upon the soul with a grip that cannot be dislodged, and the hope of the new American civilization, like that of the ancient Hebrew, is still vested in them whom God has chosen to be His prophets.

# CHAPTER XII

### GARDNER'S ARREST AND TRIAL

WE have now traversed with a good deal of detail, the four months of 1892 following upon the initial sermon preached in February of that year. The lines were now distinctly drawn and the battle fairly on. Each of the two opponents had learned pretty well to know his adversary, and it was beginning to be felt that the battle would not cease except with the complete defeat of one or the other of the combatants. The ground has, in the preceding chapters, been laid out with so much of definiteness that from this time on our narrative can proceed with much greater rapidity. Very little worthy of record transpired during the summer months of '92. Our Society suffered sadly in the loss by death in July of Mr. David J. Whitney, an indefatigable and fearless worker in the cause, a member of the Executive Committee, and one of the charter members of the Board. The vacancy thus created in the Executive Committee was filled by the election of Frank Moss, Esq., who had been, since 1887, the Society's attorney.

At this point in the narrative better than at any other, perhaps, it is my pleasure as well as duty to recognize the services which have been rendered by Messrs. T. D. Kenneson and Frank Moss, as members of the Executive Committee of the Society for the Prevention of Crime. The community has no appreciation of the amount of time and effort which have been expended by these two gentlemen in the interests of our city during the years past. There is altogether too much disposition to bestow the credit of the issue upon the President of the Society, and vastly too little recognition of the fact that if he has been able to accomplish anything, it is because of the wise and tireless support of these two colleagues. Our relations have been those of unbroken harmony. Our mutual confidence has been complete, and all questions of moment have been decided by our combined judgment.

Neither will it be considered by Mr. Kenneson as unjust to himself if I emphasize especially the faithful service rendered by Mr. Moss. His relation as attorney to the Society involved a special draft upon his time and energy. It ought to be understood by our citizens that during all the years that he has served the city, devoting to it sometimes for many days together, his entire energy, he has not received a dollar of compensation ; indeed, the terms of our Constitution forbid that the services of any member should be remunerated (except by the love of our friends and the hatred of our enemies). Mr. Moss has had long experience in dealing with the viciousness of our Police, and it was with reference to this matter that the late Dr. Crosby was writing under date of July 26, 1887, when he said: "Whatever may be the issue of the Williams matter, Mr. Moss has established a reputation for wisdom, boldness, and energy, which any lawyer might covet. He will be known by the public as a resolute defender of the City's purity."

Aside from the three members of the Executive Committee already specified, the following gentlemen have been prominently and officially connected with the Society, and devoted to its interests during the last three years:

David J. Whitney,* William A. Harding, William H. Arnoux, Edward A. Newell, Henry M. MacCracken, Abbott E. Kittredge, Thaddeus D. Kenneson, Frank Moss, Lewis L. Delafield, William C. Stuart, J. N. Hallock, Hiram Hitchcock, Noah Davis.

Great injustice would be done did we not also mention the members of our detective force, upon whose integrity, fidelity, and skill we have depended in all the executive work of the Society; who have exposed themselves to peril and obloquy, but who have identified their interests with our own, and to whom, therefore, the gratitude of the public as well as of our Society is due for the results which have been accom-

* Deceased.

plished. Those especially deserving honorable mention are the following :

John H. Lemmon, Edgar A. Whitney, Arthur F. Dennet, Benjamin F. Nott, Martin Van Ryn, Henry Burr.

Our detective force during the autumn of 1892 was small, and most of the work was done by C. W. Gardner. He understood well, however, the field in which he was employed by us to operate, and was by this means a continuous irritation to the goldbanded and brass-buttoned characters among whom his services were rendered.

It was natural enough, therefore, for Superintendent Byrnes to think it an important part of his official duty to interpose as many obstacles as possible to our Society's activity. There is nothing to show that either he, or any of his subordinates, has spent so many anxious days or watchful nights over any matter as they have over the sincere attempts which we have been making for the past three years to diminish the volume of crime.

An instance of the above occurred near the end of November of that year, as appears from the following, taken from the *Herald* of the 30th of that month : " A rule will be reported at the next meeting of the Board of Police Justices, which provides that hereafter, warrants shall be issued only to persons who are authorized by law to execute the same. This rule will prevent agents of the Rev. Dr. Parkhurst's Society from executing warrants as heretofore.

"The matter was brought to the attention of the Police Commissioners by Superintendent Byrnes, who represented that the habit of issuing warrants to irresponsible parties ought to be stopped.

" Dr. Parkhurst in speaking of the matter last night said : ' This has been a fair and square fight all the way through between the people whom Superintendent Byrnes represents and the people we represent. I fully understand that when Mr. Byrnes suggested that change in the matter of issuing warrants, it was a blow aimed at us. Mr. Byrnes and his followers have no love for us, and, without mincing matters, I think I may say that we reciprocate the feeling heartily.

"' I am glad this change has been made, because it separates us, and that influential part of the community we represent, from those whom we wish to fight. And we shall go right on fighting them, too, and the more obstacles they place in our path, the worse it will be for them, for we shall spare no pains to put the public in possession of the facts. So that this fight, which they are making against us, is going to strengthen our cause rather than weaken it.' "

We are not at this point raising any question as to the wisdom of the rule proposed by Superintendent Byrnes, we are only calling attention to the fact that it was he that moved in the matter, and that the immediate effect of that rule when adopted, would be to embarrass the operations of our detectives ; it merely occurs to us to ask whether inasmuch as he was drafting rules to obstruct our detectives, it would not have been eminently commendatory for him at the same time to have drafted some rules that would have obstructed the criminal operations of some of his own detectives. I speak of them here as criminal because they have been shown to be such by the Lexow Committee. Is it that he enjoyed the criminality of his detectives more than he did that of our own ? Or that he gave more interested and concerned attention to the movements of our detectives than he did to his ?

The next move in the same direction was the arrest of Detective Gardner, less than a week later, that is, December 4th. This was one of the severest blows ever experienced by our Society, and yet in the issue, as we shall soon see, made larger contributions than any other single cause to the grand overthrow of last November; it is for that reason that some space needs to be accorded to it in any thorough account of our three years' work. This is no place to discuss the question of Gardner's guilt or innocence ; all that in this connection we shall have any interest to say about the case will hold with equal force whichever of the two alternatives the reader may choose to adopt. Although in justice to Mr. Gardner, it ought to be said that scarcely anyone, outside of Gardner himself, is as qualified as the Executive Committee of the Society for the Prevention of Crime to arrive at a safe conclusion upon the question, and neither one of the three members of that committee has the suggestion of a suspicion of Gardner's guilt. I might add, also, that our conviction is shared in by the crooks and thugs of the town—parties whose moral sense is certainly badly blunted, but who necessarily become expert in tracking the devices of the police, and exceptionally qualified to interpret their motives and methods.

The charge brought against Mr. Gardner was that of attempted blackmail; he was accused of trying to extort protection money from the keeper of a vile resort. The Police Department, from centre to circumference, was stirred by the vast possibilities of the case. We are speaking within bounds when we say that not for many years have the energies of the entire Department been so concentrated in securing the conviction of a reputed criminal. It hardly needs to be said, in view of the late developments of the Lexow Committee, that that was not because of any antipathy to blackmail. The police objected to Gardner's blackmailing anyone for the reason that they wanted the monopoly of the business themselves, and were anxious to secure his conviction, because they thought that in convicting him they would be convicting and paralyzing our Society, and thus be destroying the only obstacle they knew of to the continuance of the blackmailing operations in which they were themselves engaged. Aside from the defendant, the conspicuous actors in the drama of Gardner's conviction and prosecution, were the prostitute Clifton, Recorder Smyth, and Captain Devery. It is a queer commentary on the animus of the whole transaction, that the prostitute is now under indictment, that Smyth was indicted at the polls on the 6th of November (in part because of his demeanor in this very prosecution), and Devery has been discharged from the Police Service for conduct unbecoming an officer. In view of all this, it is not very difficult to judge how much of Gardner's arrest and conviction was due to a fine moral enthusiasm, and how much of it was damnable conspiracy.

If in the way in which the thing has just been presented there is a tinge of bitterness, we can conscientiously declare that that sentiment is not due to the fact of Gardner's arrest and conviction, but to the fact that, even granting Gardner's guilt, he was doing just that which Byrnes, Devery, and all their associates knew the entire Police Department to be engaged in — levying blackmail — and that their stupendous and organized scheme to "down" Gardner was simply a sublime effort to bolster up official iniquity, and that their colossal laments over the "Fall of poor Gardner" were a clever, though sneaking device, for disguising habitual and systematic corruption of their own.

Gardner was not arrested by Mr. Byrnes and his subordinates because he was a criminal, but because he was our detective, and because he made it more difficult for Mr. Byrnes's department to act out its own remunerative depravity. We knew all this at the time ; subsequent developments have enabled the rest of community to know it.

The blow dealt by Gardner's arrest was a shrewd one. Temporarily it discredited the Society for the Prevention of Crime in the public estimate. Our cause was not going to prevail until matters had reached that stage where temporary defeat on our part was not going to shake the town's confidence. That time came, but not till a little later. On the 5th of December the Society for the Prevention of Crime stock was very low and continued falling for months. Our citizens trusted us in seasons of good weather but not between times.

One of the first effects of Gardner's arrest was that the Executive Committee came together and agreed to strengthen our detective force. Money it was hard to obtain, and members of the Society advanced the requisite funds. A good deal of our interest and attention was necessarily devoted for a time to Gardner's trial, but the purposes of the Executive Committee were, under this adverse experience, toughened into more strenuous determination, and our transient adversity both put us upon defining more sharply our own lines of action and upon securing detectives sufficient in character, calibre, and number to prosecute those lines. In point of effectiveness we were in finer shape shortly subsequent to Gardner's arrest than we had ever been before. How much we owe to the vicious opposition of the enemy !

It will be impossible to go into the details of Gardner's trial, which opened on January 30, 1893. It was felt by all who had any appreciation of the situation, that the contesting parties who appeared in the suit were representatives simply, and that the real plaintiff and defendant were nothing less than the two great elements of our municipality that were striving for mastery, two great systems of administration that aimed at nothing less than each other's overthrow. It was not Gardner that we were trying to defend, nor was it Gardner that they were trying to convict. The sense of this intensified all proceedings, and explains much of the passionate interest with which the case was watched, and the passionate energy with which it was conducted. In that trial the Police Department, from the Commissioners down, was distinctly conscious of its direct antagonism to that entire element in community which demanded an honest maintenance of honest laws and of the common weal. That consciousness explained the large and eager attendance of high police officials, and was distinctly manifested in the demeanor of Recorder Smyth, who sat on the Bench and who was known to be the close personal friend of Superintendent Byrnes. One of the leaders of the New York Bar some days since stated that, in his opinion, it was Smyth's intention to have Gardner convicted. If this was the case, it only goes to show how much we had to contend with in trying to make head against a combination of Police, Demi

Monde, and Judiciary. But what is quite as interesting is that this same member of the Bar just quoted, went on to remark that the Recorder's bearing on this occasion (such as his mode of dealing with the counsel for the defence, and his repeated prompting of the disreputable Clifton while on the witness stand) disturbed the confidence which the Bar had had in Recorder Smyth's judicial integrity, or at least their confidence in his judicial equipoise. In this way the Recorder's prodigal use of the power of his position (or what an observant public considered to be such) stands in intimate relation with the move which the City has just succeeded in making to throw him out of his position, and to put a better upon the Bench in his stead.

And what is still more interesting is that the man by whom the city has just replaced Smyth is exactly the man against whom Smyth on this very occasion made special display of judicial and prejudicial power —John W. Goff. This is one of the most startling instances known to us of the revenges wrought by time. Mr. Goff fought valiantly and fearlessly in behalf of what he considered to be the rights of his client. Smyth took judicial offence at the bluntness of Mr. Goff's language, adjudged him in contempt and fined him $200; but a higher court than that of Smyth sat on the 6th of November last, which invited Mr. Smyth to step down and Mr. Goff to move up to his place. In behalf of the New York Bar,

Joseph H. Choate, Esq., made a plea before the Recorder in Mr. Goff's interest, the distinguishing feature of which was that while there was nettle enough in it to sting the Recorder's nerves, the nettle was rubbed in with such polished courtesy that the poor victim had to behave as though he were being dosed with the Balm of Gilead.

It is not pertinent to the main object of our story to dwell upon the matter of Mr. Gardner's conviction and sentence, his temporary confinement in the Tombs and subsequent release, the reversal of the Recorder's judgment, the carrying of the case to the Court of Appeals, and the final ordering of a new trial. It is enough for our purpose to have shown that his arrest and trial accomplished four most important and healthful results: It brought about the reorganization and strengthening of our office; it suggested to the community, under startling colors, the organized combination seeming to exist between the police, the prostitutes, and the Bench; it prepared for the defeat of Recorder Smyth; and last and best of all, it cordially introduced to the knowledge and confidence of this community, our coadjutor, John W. Goff.

# CHAPTER XIII

### THE SOCIAL EVIL

THE Social Evil has played an important part in the history of our work, and far more important than it would have done had not the intent of the movement been, at the outset, quite generally misapprehended, and had not the Police Department utilized that misapprehension to the end of discrediting our efforts, and thereby breaking the force of our attack. Our reference to the matter here is not made with any intention of discussing the problem which it involves. We have steadily avoided being drawn into any argument in reference to it, and that for two reasons; first, our crusade was not a crusade against sexual vice or any other vice; our warfare was only against the police considered as the salaried protectors of vice. And we have felt that for us to discuss the proper method of dealing with the Social Evil would be only to confuse the issue and to side-track the entire movement. If we commenced our crusade by the visitation of disorderly houses, it was only because that was the easiest means by which police indifference to blatant crime in this city could be brought to light and made public.

The second reason why it is unwise for us or for anyone else to discuss just now the proper method of handling the Social Evil in this city, is that, as yet, the conditions here are not such as to make the discussion worth the breath that is expended upon it. The present extent of the evil is no measure of what it would be under normal conditions, and we cannot consider the question intelligently till normal conditions are reached. What we mean is this: that social vice has been so protected and encouraged by the filthy officials who control the department, that the number of abandoned women and disorderly houses now existing in the city is no measure of what it would be if we had a police force, from top down, who conceived of sexual crime as an evil to be suppressed, not as capital to draw dividend from. I have had women of this class tell me in my own house that they did not belong here, but that they came here from outside because they knew that in New York the police would protect them. That fact is known all over. The police of this city have been enticing prostitutes from other cities and States to come to New York, in order that they might be the means of clothing their own wives and daughters and living in style, quadrupling in comfort and elegance anything they could maintain on their legitimate salaries. It will, therefore, be time to discuss the Social Evil when we have police officials whose ambition it is to reduce, not extend, the number of prostitutes, and when that number, therefore, falls to its normal figure.

The efforts we have made to demonstrate the criminal negligence of the police have resulted indirectly in the raiding of a great many houses which it formed no part of our plan to disturb. And the brutality with which such raids have often been conducted has been steadily availed of by the police, and by our enemies outside of the force, to embarrass and discredit our work. But with all of the misunderstanding that was occasioned in this way, and purposely promoted, there is no room to doubt that an unprecedentedly large number of unfortunate women have, during the past two years, been brought to realize not only the precariousness of their mode of life but its essential degradation.

There is in our city deep interest in this question, and I venture to introduce here a statement of the cases of three or four of the very large number of young women who have recently been led by the disturbed condition of affairs to abandon their disreputable life, and who have come to us for counsel and help. I have, for the past fourteen months, employed a young woman with special reference to working among this class of people, and the statements subjoined are given largely in her words:

" K. S—— is an interesting case. She came from Cherry Street, where she had lived three years as an abandoned woman. She says she used often to wish she could get out of her life, but she had no place to go in the repentant moods, and then she would harden her heart again and make herself think she did not want to go. When the house in which she was living was raided, she was compelled to go. She sat on the doorstep of her former home, wondering what she was to do now that she had been forced into the street, when suddenly it came to her like a flash that perhaps this was for the best after all, and perhaps she could be good again, and turn from the old wicked life. She was taken in at the Mission at which she applied, and is happy there, and has already come forward desiring to be converted. She was one of the most sinful and degraded type. She told the Mission friends that she had drunk eight gallons of whiskey in three days, and she was very ill with delirium tremens on her arrival. But for the seeming misfortune which shut her off from her old means of gaining a livelihood, she would still be deep in her old life of sin and degradation."

" L. L—— is another interesting girl, educated, gentle, and lady-like. She came from the South about six months ago with a man who had betrayed her. After a day or two in the city she entered a disreputable house. At the end of three or four weeks she was overcome with disgust at the life she was living, but, a stranger in the city, and without friends, she did not know what to do or where to go. She had been in the house six months when it was raided. She happened to be there at the time, and was arrested and sent to jail for ten days.

While in the jail a missionary came to her, and the girl begged her to help her leave the old life. She was taken to one of the 'Homes,' and is now there. Nothing, she says, would induce her to return to the sinful life she has learned to detest. 'I thank Dr. Parkhurst from the bottom of my heart,' she said."

"M. T—— was well educated and had money enough at home, but was betrayed while visiting a friend. After that her downfall was rapid. She began to drink and drank heavily, and went rapidly from bad to worse until she was finally found in a saloon, after one of the recent raids, half-desperate, half-repentant, and a hand was held out to her just in time. She said that she had been turned out of her house into the streets, and though she hated those who had done her this apparent injury, it had made her, for the first time in a long while, think what she was doing, and she began to long for a different life. She, too, has been provided for, and is being watched by interested friends who desire to help her."

Our missionary says there is a general sense of injury among the girls who are turned out, but it is because they misunderstand the motives of the whole movement. They say, "It is all very well to close the houses, but to turn us out into the streets, homeless and penniless, is terrible." They do not know that Dr. Parkhurst will provide for all who desire to leave the old life, and that they can obtain food and shelter simply by asking for it. When this is explained to them they say, "Oh, that's different." The policemen turn them against the Doctor. All the girls in the Homes are doing well, and all say that but for the trouble which drove them into the street they would never have been able to cut loose from the old life. Two girls said to our missionary, "Well, I would never have left it myself, for what else was there for me to do?" Some of the girls are surprisingly well educated and gentle in their manner, though the life is so terribly degrading it soon kills their better side. It is a curious fact that not one passes under her own name, the name of her father and mother, but assumes a name as soon as she enters the life."

Another lady having a large experience with this class of women says :

" There are more ' rounders ' (the homeless creatures who have wandered for years in the streets) that have beds this winter than ever before, and more meals given them. In all my long experience in the work, I have never known such efforts to be put forth by Christian people as this winter. Dr. Parkhurst and his glorious work has stirred everybody up. If he has done nothing else, he has waked up the Christian Churches. It is making the girls stop to think, and it has certainly given vice a severe set-back. It is no longer open and daring.''

" B. H—— had lived a fast life for the past six years, a drunkard and a fallen girl. She lived at one time with Mrs. ——, of — Delancey Street. She would gladly have left her sinful life long ago, but lacked courage to come out from her old companions. Four weeks ago the house was closed, but after a week she returned to the house and was taken in again, and for a week led the same life. Two weeks ago, Sunday night, Captain Cortright came and closed the place again. She then thought of her former days when she was a pure girl, and resolved to do right. December 24th she came to the Florence Mission, and since then has showed every sign of being a changed girl. Her heart goes out in gratitude that God allowed her to be thrown out of her old life, and that He has saved her from a drunkard's grave."

"A. B——, when first turned out of her old life, was directed to Dr. Parkhurst by a saloon-keeper, who told her that he had already sent one girl there, and that she had been placed in a 'Home.' On first leaving the house where she had been staying, she told a man whom she met on the street that she was going to Dr. Parkhurst. He told her that she was a fool to go, that Dr. Parkhurst sent all the girls that applied to him to the Island for four months. So she did nothing till she met the saloon-keeper, who urged her to go, and assured her that Dr. Parkhurst did help the girls who came to him anxious to lead a new life, and that she could be sure of a welcome from him."

It has been something of a trial to know that at the very time we were trying to provide food and homes for the girls that the police were throwing out into the street, the Police Commissioners or their pals were trying to make it appear that we were responsible for police brutality, and that the object of our movement was to occasion the poor girls the largest possible annoyance and privation. The mistake the police finally made was in overdoing the matter, and this occurred, particularly in the "Tenderloin," early in December of 1893. In the midst of a bitter cold night, the police went through the district making general havoc, driving the girls out into the snow, and with a vicious malignity, in which they are experts, gave the terror-stricken victims to understand that this was all of it the doings of "Old Parkhurst." Indeed the girls were allowed to understand that the raiding was being done by detectives of our own Society.

My house was literally besieged with the poor, hungry unfortunates who came, a part of them to get food from me, and a still larger part to damn me. People are even yet sometimes expressing surprise that I have so little admiration and respect for our police force! I believe that from top down, with some splendid exceptions, they are the dirtiest, crookedest, and ugliest lot of men ever combined in semi-military array outside of Japan and Turkey.

The "Tenderloin" business, however, was overdone, and wrought its own fine reaction. It soon became noised abroad that we had not had a detective in the "Tenderloin" precinct for months, and the curses began gradually to roll off from our shoulders onto those of the blue-coated brutes to which they belonged;

and it then, for the first time, began to be understood throughout the ranks of the unfortunate women that it was the police that were persecuting the women, and that what we were in pursuit of was the police.

I sent out the following letter, which, by the courtesy of the press, was printed in the morning journals of December 9th :

*To the Editor of* ——.

Sir : It having come to my knowledge that a considerable number of women have, by the action of the police, been suddenly thrown out upon the streets, may I avail myself of the courtesy of your columns to say that I shall gladly render all needed assistance to any of them who may desire to abandon their old ways and return to a life that is pure and womanly. We are sorry to have anyone suffer, and yet, of course, our offer can be made only to such as have a purpose of forsaking their criminal relations, and this offer we cordially and affectionately extend, not only to those who have been recently evicted, but to any women anywhere in the town who are at present living in houses of the description of those just closed, but who are anxious to change their condition, and to adopt a mode of life that is honorable and self-respecting. We are gratified that our motives as a Society are, in this respect, becoming better understood, and while, of course, we shall go on with increased steadfastness in our work of making it difficult for the police to hold over these women a hand of criminal protection, we shall be just as constant in our efforts to afford Christian protection from hunger and exposure to any who may desire to enter the ways of virtue and honorable self-support.

   (Signed)   C. H. PARKHURST,
      President of the Society for the
       Prevention of Crime.

A public appeal was also made for money, and handsomely responded to. The raiding went on in that same wild way which regularly characterizes the action of the police, when there *is* any action, and the girls came to our house in droves. The various "Homes" of the city opened their doors promptly and hospitably, and no one was allowed to suffer who showed any desire to meet us frankly, and to return to a life of purity and womanliness.

The results of this can be seen in a large number of young women, some of them still resident here, others returned to their homes in the country, one even studying to be a missionary, who are now living honorable lives, and who, with purified and grateful hearts are honoring God and blessing mankind, lamenting the past, but making it an incentive to watchfulness in the present and womanly effort for the future.

This whole event, interesting as it may be as a chapter in the moral history of the city, specially concerns us here only because of its effect in helping our criminal and distressed classes to understand the spirit of our movement; it enabled them to come at the fact from a new stand-point, that not ourselves, but the Tammany police were their real persecutors, and so was one of the influences contributing to the successful effort at emancipation made by them on the 6th of last November.

# CHAPTER XIV

## BYRNES'S EFFORT TO DISCREDIT THE CRUSADE

SUPERINTENDENT, Inspectors, Captains and Commissioners had been expecting that the "storm would blow over." On the contrary, there were growing signs of the storm's becoming chronic, and it appears to have been thought that some stalwart move must be vigorously made looking to the clearing of the air, and that some summary blow must be dealt that would abruptly silence and crush out the Society for the Prevention of Crime and its following.

Two blows were delivered in quick succession, both of them with the design of crippling the Society, in the one instance by discrediting the Society's detective, Gardner, in the other by discrediting the Society's President.

Detective Gardner was arrested on December 4, 1892. Byrnes undertook to crush me on December 6th. He used Devery and a prostitute to pulverize Gardner, and the reporters to blacken me. Reference is made to this matter of the Byrnes correspondence, in the first place, for the reason that it forms an important chapter in the history of the three years; and again for the reason that it will give community an opportunity to acquaint itself afresh with the quality and genius of the unique personality under whose supervision our police force has reached its present phenomenal stage of development, and under whose supervision, if the will of his accomplices and admirers could be done, that same police force would secure its reorganization. According to the reports printed at the time, Mr. Byrnes seems to have pondered his verbal assault upon me with considerable deliberation, and to have called the representatives together at his office in order that his challenge might be both widely and correctly published. The matter of it appeared in the morning papers of December 7th. As reported in the *Herald* of that date, it reads as follows :

"'No quarter for Parkhurst.' So in substance said Superintendent Byrnes at ten o'clock last night, when, in his private office at Police Headquarters, he launched a thunder-bolt by which he hopes to crush the ministerial crusader."

"'Now, gentlemen,' said he, 'I had intended to issue to-night a full and complete statement of facts in reply to statements made in a general way against the Police Department of this city by the Rev. Dr. Parkhurst. I find, however, that to complete the statement to-night will be impossible. It will be ready for you probably to-morrow.

"'I have, however, this to say at once for publication. Never before have I criticised Dr. Parkhurst.

but now I flatly challenge his motives, and declare that he makes statements against the Department I represent, without evidence to support them and without belief in them himself.

"'This so-called crusade of the Doctor, I am now prepared to state, was started by him and several well-known members of his congregation, with motives of revenge against this Department bred by a policeman's refusal to testify to suit them in a certain divorce suit. That suit was brought by a young member of Dr. Parkhurst's church against her husband. The Doctor and several influential parishioners rallied around her, and because the policeman refused to testify to order, they invented this alleged crusade.

"'The divorce was finally secured, and then promptly followed the Doctor's historic call on Hattie Adams. Masked though it was, that was the beginning of the attack by Parkhurst and his church followers upon the Police Department. Now, gentlemen, I come to the gist of the whole business,' and the Superintendent paused for an instant as though to freshly consider the important statements to follow.

"'Reluctantly I say this much. I have letters in my possession showing conclusively that Parkhurst and certain members of his church are banded together to secure evidence compromising to the highest officials in this city.

"'These letters further show that Parkhurst and his associates resort to means that seem most dishonorable to accomplish this purpose. By intrigues with women, their paid stool-pigeons, they seek to compromise the Chief Magistrate of the city, our prosecuting officer, a number of judges, and prominent municipal officials. Their names appear in the letters now in my possession, copies of which I have had prepared for use in the complete statement I am preparing for publication.'

"The Superintendent paused for breath and then went to work again on his ministerial foe:

"'These letters,' said he, 'will show the instructions left by Parkhurst when he went abroad—instructions left to be carried out by his co-workers during his absence in Europe. They are written for the most part by the mother of the woman whose divorce suit caused all the trouble, and detail the intrigues of the band up to within a few days of the present time.

"'No, no,' hastily replied the Superintendent in response to a request for the woman's name, 'I'll not tell you. Parkhurst can. Ask him. Her daughter secured the divorce about nine months ago, and the mother — Parkhurst's most scheming assistant and personal friend—is away up socially, I can tell you.

"'Every letter is to a person with whom an interview was had. In these interviews public men were named, as I am prepared to prove, as victims for some compromising intrigue to be worked by a woman.'

"Closing the rolling top of his desk with a bang, the

Superintendent rose from his chair with the abrupt announcement :

"'There, gentlemen, that is all for to-night. Ask all the questions you care to, but expect no further information until I am ready to make public the complete statement.'

"The questions were plied thick and fast upon the doughty 'Chief,' who coolly slipped into his overcoat and stepped to the door with a pleasant 'Good-night.' Not a name would he give or an additional particular, but as his hand touched the door-knob he turned on his questioners.

"'Well, boys,' said he, ' I will tell you one thing more to show the contemptible character of this man Parkhurst. After the arrest of Hattie Adams, and while her trial was pending, Parkhurst asked this letter-writing mother of a divorced daughter to get him some of the most abominable French pictures that are fugitive in this market. His friend and co-laborer readily consented, and with another woman secured the beastly prints and took them in great glee to her pastor. Parkhurst's object in securing them was to offer them as pictorial evidence of the scenes he had witnessed in the Adams house.

"'When, however, his faithful parishioner delivered them, the wily Doctor hesitated.

"'Suppose,' said he, 'that some inquisitive juror asks me how the pictures came in my possession? That would be embarrassing. To obviate anything of that kind, please take the prints away with you and send them to me by mail in an envelope. Purely anonymous, see? Then, ladies, I can conscientiously swear that they were sent to me by some one entirely unknown.'

"'It was done. Now, that gives you an idea of Parkhurst's high character.'"

I submitted my reply to the reporters the same evening, which was as follows:

"There came to my notice this morning a statement purporting to have emanated from Superintendent Byrnes touching the animus and method of the work in which I have been engaged during the past ten months. The statement, presumably authentic, is an attempt on his part to extricate himself from an awkward position by trying to put me in another awkward position of a similar character. He is trying to blacken me as a means of whitewashing himself and his Department.

"Now, for the sake of argument, I am going, for the instant, to plead guilty to his entire indictment. I am going to assume that my motives have been villainous from the start; that, as he intimates, I have been actuated now for almost a year by a sheer spirit of revenge; that something transpiring in a certain 'divorce case' so embittered me that I have been spending all these months in the attempt to square myself with the Department.

"Well, supposing all that is true, what of it? How

does that help Mr. Byrnes any? Does that fact close up any of the gambling-houses that he is allowing to run? Suppose I have been dealing in 'French pictures' and that I had all my pockets full of them when I went into the court-room on a special occasion, what of it? Does that fact suppress any of the vile dens of infamy in this city which exist because Mr. Byrnes and his Department are viciously neglectful of their duty?

"Supposing I have availed of members of my congregation, availed of all of them, and put them upon the track of city officials, set them studying up the unwholesome record of any who are to-day in positions of municipal authority, and arranged with all my elders, deacons, and deaconesses to discover the facts as to the domestic life of the Police Commissioners, police magistrates, and police captains, what of it? How does that help Mr. Byrnes? In what way does the fact of such an arrangement operate to neutralize that other fact of the recognized existence in this city of institutions for the practice of unnatural vices?

"Mr. Byrnes is trying to shift the issue from his shoulders to mine. He is in a hard place and he is tired! He thinks that by showing the community what I am doing he will make the community forget what he isn't doing. It is shrewdly designed, but too transparent to prove a success.

"To touch now two or three specific points in Mr. Byrnes's letter. A picture was in my pocket on the morning of the Andrea trial which I was planning to show the jury in case it seemed that it should be more effective than oral description. When the time came I judged that oral evidence would do the work best and the picture was withheld.

"As to availing myself of detectives to shadow some of our city officials during the summer while I was away, that was done, and well done. It was done in the exercise of a distinct right which I have, not as President of the Society for the Prevention of Crime simply, but in the right which I have as a citizen. We have gone quite too long without watching our city officials, and that is part of the difficulties we are suffering under to-day. If the exigency arrives again, I shall put detectives on the track of the officials again, and if I think circumstances are such as require it I shall put a detective on Mr. Byrnes. If he is doing right it won't hurt him. If he isn't doing right he ought not to object if it does hurt him. Mr. Byrnes is one of our municipal servants. I am helping to pay his salary.

"His opposition to having our public officials watched has a bad look. I have been shadowed off and on for the last nine months.

"Touching the matter of the 'divorce case' and its relations to the work of my Society during the past year, Mr. Byrnes says, 'His attack originated in a divorce case about nine months ago.' That statement is totally and unredeemably false to the last dot. It was not even the occasion of my attack. It was not even an incident of my attack. It had nothing to do with it in any way, shape, or manner. Mr. Byrnes continues: 'Dr. Parkhurst was interested in the case. They wanted a police officer to testify to certain facts which he could not conscientiously swear to and he refused. Dr. Parkhurst showed his anger at that time.' I have not the slightest recollection of any such event, and so far from the refusal of a policeman to perjure himself exciting my anger, it would only have excited in me devout thanksgiving.

"Mr. Byrnes says, 'I do not believe Dr. Parkhurst is sincere in his talk.' I am not going to attempt to prove my sincerity. I know what the public sentiment is on that point. There are many people in the community who question the wisdom of my methods, but I dare to say that the community does not question my sincerity. Mr. Byrnes knows that I am sincere, and if he stands in any attitude of enmity toward me that is the reason of it.

"There remains one charge in Mr. Byrnes's indictment that I cannot dismiss quite so summarily. He says that I 'have continued to make accusations without evidence.' The colossal impudence of that accusation is well-nigh paralyzing. Permit me to address half a dozen sentences to the Superintendent directly: Mr. Byrnes, are you familiar with the terms of Section 282 of the Act of Consolidation? Are you knowing to the fact that that section makes it obligatory upon you and your Department to make yourselves acquainted with all places in this city where gambling is being carried on and disorderly houses maintained, and 'to repress and restrain all unlawful or disorderly conduct or practices therein, to enforce and prevent the violation of all laws and ordinances in force in said city?'

"Now, Mr. Byrnes, what have I and my Society been doing all these ten months from the time when I presented those affidavits from the pulpit of my church, but piling up before the community the proofs of the persistent neglect of your Department to discharge the duties the above section makes obligatory upon you? What is the meaning of the existence of such a Society as that for the Prevention of Crime or for the Suppression of Vice if it is not that the police fail just at the point where their services ought to be rendered?

"Every disorderly house that we have pulled, and that you ought to have pulled, every gambling-house that we have frightened into closing its doors, and whose doors, sir, you yourself were the proper person to have closed, is a standing indictment against you and against the integrity and efficiency of the police service.

"I have seen it stated within a few days that you have said that Dr. Parkhurst has never been to see you to get your help; that you were in a condition to render me a good deal of service, but that I have never sought your assistance. Sought your assistance!

Why, Mr. Byrnes, do you not know that it is the criminal neglect of your Department which is the one thing we are fighting? You can help us to close brothels, no doubt, but that is not what we are trying to do. We are trying to make it so hot for you that you will close them yourself. We are not trying to suppress gambling, nor trying to suppress the social evil. We are trying to suppress your own criminal neglect of the duties which the above-quoted section devolves upon you and upon every member of your department.

"Permit me, Mr. Byrnes, to bid you remember that the presentment of the March Grand Jury of 1892 still hangs over your department very much in the nature of an indictment. Don't attempt, sir, to transfer the burden of the situation from your shoulders to mine. I make no claim to superior merit. However many vices I may have, conceit is not one of them, but I do say that I am standing with all my might, and the might of my Society, for the honest execution of wholesome laws in this city, and, strong in that consciousness and fresh from the reading of pitiful complaints, this whole island over, of fathers, mothers, and sisters, who are pouring in upon me their appeals for protection against the blatant iniquity that prevails in our streets, it makes my blood boil, sir, to see you bringing to bear upon me, for the purposes of discredit, that machinery of your department which, as a man and an officer, it is your prerogative as well as your obligation to make effective to the aid of the tempted and the relief of the distressed.

"The issue between us now is definite, and yet the issue is not between you and me. It is between two classes in the community, of which you and I happen just now to be the representatives. It is an issue between criminal rule on the one side and honest rule on the other. It is a battle between purity and lechery. It is a fight between true citizens who pay honest money for the administration of municipal government, and the criminals in and out of office to whom government means nothing but opportunity to feed and fatten on the common treasury and the general life. It is well now that lines have been sharply drawn. It simplifies the struggle and will hasten the issue."

The community understands now, as it did not then, the unspeakable greediness and almost unmentionable vileness of which Mr. Byrnes was the executive head. He was acquainted with the character of the police force at that time, or he was not acquainted with it. If he was not acquainted with it he stands thereby convicted of base negligence or of colossal incompetence. If he was acquainted with it, his assault upon our efforts to improve the force was sneaking, vicious and malignant.

## CHAPTER XV

#### FIRST ATTACK ON DEVERY

DETECTIVE GARDNER had been convicted early in February. It was a hard blow for us, but we succeeded in continuing cheerful. Our work for some months was conducted with considerable quietness. Byrnes doubtless imagined that his two blows dealt in quick succession had confused our purposes and paralyzed our hopes. We made almost no overt movement that would tend to excite his suspicion that anything of an aggressive nature was being contemplated by us. We worked, however, industriously but on the quiet.

Our experiences of twelve months (for Gardner was convicted just a year after the delivery of my first sermon), had given us a fairly clear understanding of the field and of the temper of our enemy. We never for one moment entertained the thought of abandoning the enterprise or of compromising with them. Several overtures were made us through intermediaries, looking to a cessation of hostilities and to an alliance with the police, all of which were promptly and unequivocally declined and resented; and it may as well be said at this point that whatever contribution the

Society for the Prevention of Crime made to the recent overthrow of Tammany Hall, it made by virtue of its refusal to stand toward Byrnes or any of his superiors or subordinates in any other relation than that of sworn enemy.

In those quiet weeks and months, however, there was being a good deal done. We gathered together a force of detectives of whose work the Society may well be proud. In only one instance, I believe, did we err in our man, and even in his case the treason to our interests was distinctly due to his having been tampered with at Police Headquarters, as is proved by his affidavit, which we hold in our possession. If these lines should happen to fall under the eye of Inspector Williams, his cultivated perspicacity will doubtless be able to penetrate our allusion. The public will find, in this reference, another indication of the difficulties against which we had to contend, and of the concealed pit-falls into which we were constantly liable to tumble.

With our office thus interiorly strengthened and compacted, we laid out a scheme of long, detailed, and careful work. We were in no haste. Our principle was that what was worth working for at all was worth working for a good while. The Executive Committee agreed that our next step must be to make a solid case of malfeasance against a police captain. Before fixing upon a candidate for our Society's attention, we devoted a considerable period of investigation to the condition and workings of a number of precincts that had been reported to us as exceptionally bad, and fixed finally upon the Eleventh, Captain Devery's, as being the one where there was not only as much tolerated, not to say protected crime, as in any other, but as being the precinct where, as it appeared to our detectives, gambling and disorderly resorts were being conducted with a more shameless and blatant openness than in any other. Besides this, the Eleventh Precinct has the reputation of being one whose market value was quite as high as that of any other, which was understood to mean that Captain Devery had to pay roundly for his precinct, and that his criminal business had consequently to be stimulated so that it could pay roundly for his reimbursement.

For a number of weeks, then, our work was limited to the Eleventh Precinct, which is situated on the East and lower side of the town, and bounded by Houston, Clinton, Rivington, Norfolk, and Division Streets, and the Bowery.

We had kept careful record of all letters of complaint written us respecting criminal resorts in that and other precincts, and had received, besides, occasional assistance from residents in that quarter of the town, whose indignation overcame their fears, and made them willing to run the risk of allying themselves with our cause. As a rule, however, the reign of terror was so ruthlessly maintained by the police, that until recently little information has reached us except of an anonymous kind.

Starting out with the lines thus furnished, our detectives made themselves, in a detailed way, master of a portion of Devery's precinct, and before the close of May had secured sixty-four solid cases—considered such by the legal members of the executive committee—against gambling and disorderly houses. We then prepared letters of complaint addressed to the Mayor, the Police Commissioners, the Superintendent of Police, and the public, respectively; submitting copies of the same to the press for general publication. These letters were prepared before my departure for Europe in June of that year, but, for reasons not requiring to be stated here, were not transmitted to the city officials nor given to the press till the 10th of August following.

The statement addressed to the general public was as follows:—

"It has been stated by some, with whom the wish is, doubtless, parent to the thought, that the Society for the Prevention of Crime is an extinct institution. The present opportunity is availed of to say that at no time in its history has the Society been so full of purpose, or so thoroughly organized for work as at this date. Those most interested in its welfare are not men that are easily discouraged, or that are swerved from the line of their intention by any devices that may be played off upon them, or by any obstructions that may be placed upon the track by those against whom their efforts are directed.

"Nothing has occurred during the year to invalidate the statement of the March Grand Jury of 1892, to the effect that the Police Department is either incompetent or criminal, and that it is not incompetent. Not only has that charge not been invalidated this year, but much has occurred to corroborate it. Having been so situated as to know what was being done by officials who are paid once by the city for enforcing the laws, and paid again, unless all signs fail, by gamblers, strumpets, and violators of excise, for not enforcing them, it has been exceedingly interesting to observe how steadily the enforcement of law has fluctuated with the fluctuations of interest shown in the matter by community. Certain police captains will understand perfectly what is meant when I say that any movement on the part of well-intentioned citizens, or any suspicion of such a movement, is to the Police Department certain signal that it is time to make another "raid." To those who have been so circumstanced as to know what has been going on out of sight, the systematic and pretty successful efforts that have been made during the last twelve months to pull wool over the eyes of the unsophisticated, have been so transparent in their farcical character as to convert the demeanor of the Department into a sort of chronic comedy. For a number of months now, so far as any overt action on the part of the community or of our Society is concerned, the police have been left to their own gains and devices, and it has been a long time since crime, in certain portions of the city, has been so unbridled as it is to-day.

"Our investigation as a society has been for some weeks devoted, to a considerable extent, to the Eleventh Precinct. This is the district in which the dignity of the law is supposed to be maintained, and crime made perilous, by the salaried ministration of Captain William S. Devery. The statutes determining his obligations are explicit. And it is impossible to suppose that he does not appreciate within certain limits the serious responsibility of his position ; but if he has any such appreciation it is equally impossible to understand how he can traverse the streets of his diocese with an erect head, or with any remaining traces of self-respect, knowing, as he is bound to know, and as he is criminally negligent if he does not know, the reeking mass of moral filth which he is maintaining there. I know the larger number of disorderly houses that are located there, and their street addresses, and the number of vile women that ply their trade in each, and the confidence that these women have that they will not be interfered with by the Captain or his subordinates or superiors, if they continue to maintain their own part of the contract with the powers that be.

The same also I am able to state in reference to the gambling evil in the same precinct. From the street I have looked directly into some of Devery's gambling saloons, that were in full blast and running with wide open doors. Even the paraphernalia of the art were in full and easy view, with no more attempt at concealment than if it had been a drygoods store or a butcher shop. That being the case, if Devery says he is trying to clean out gambling from his precinct, he lies. Police captains of that complexion are nothing more nor less than crime-breeders. How long is it going to be before the earnest integrity of this city will take hold of this organized system of damnation and root it out? Twenty churches cannot unmake crime as fast as official complicity in the Eleventh Precinct is making it.

"Only let it be said, by the way, that Devery could not maintain this protective attitude toward crime were it not for the backing which he gets from the superior authorities to which he is amenable. He is simply one factor in a colossal organization of crime by which our unhappy city is despotized. The precinct of which we have been speaking swarms with boys and girls, and is a superb fitting school for adult depravity; it is a sort of devil's seminary, in which the vicious negligence of Devery constitutes him a kind of first trustee. I have received a score of letters from that quarter of the town, written by parents who have implored me to do something that should make the police close up those houses in order that their children on their way to and from school, might not be polluted by the filthy sights that abound in some portions of Devery's precinct. 'We have been to the captain,' they say, 'but that never does any good.'

"Devery need not be moved to expressions of resentment or profanity by these accusations. We have got the facts down in black and white, and reduced to affidavits. Little children toddle around the doors and windows from which free advertisements of lust are constantly and boldly made. There is a long row of such houses in Bayard Street, for instance, standing side by side. Devery knows where they are. Byrnes has them on his list at headquarters. It was only last week that I passed them and was solicited from every one of them. Parents all through such portions of the town are crying out against the foul tyranny that binds their children to the discipline of this loathsome tuition. Mr. Byrnes has daughters. What sort of creatures might we have expected them to become if they had been obliged to grow up within the foul environment that the head of our Police Department makes a necessary part of the training of the children that grow up in Eldridge, Forsyth, Delancey, and East Houston Streets?

"And what shall we say of the intimation if the March Grand Jury of 1892 is valid, that all this official nursing of gambling and licentiousness is for the sake of the money they can make out of it for themselves and Tammany? Honesty converted into dollars; female virtue into corner lots; and the most splendid city in our country governed by a pack of freebooters who pillage the city of the best that makes it worth governing—that is why it is difficult to break up these evils. They are not primarily due to the viciousness of the Police Department; that Department is simply one of the many tentacles by means of which, whatever lucrative commodity is afloat in the air, is drawn into Tammany's capacious maw. Gambling and licentiousness are among the springs of her supply, because gambling and licentiousness are willing to pay for being protected.

"Saloon-keepers pay for not being disturbed on Sundays. Some arrests have to be made in order to keep up appearances. The rule is that there shall be sixty-seven a Sunday. The variation from that figure, up or down, has been slight since last February. A barkeeper said a few days ago : ' It will be my turn to be arrested pretty soon. I was to have been hauled up this week, but the boss arranged to have it put off for a couple of months.' Perhaps that makes it easy to understand why it was that Tammany last winter killed the bill that proposed to give saloon-keepers a wet Sunday. It would have cut off just so much opportunity for blackmail. It is for that reason that we need not fear that Tammany will pass a law for licensing gambling or prostitution.

"There is no end to this matter. People, however, are getting their eyes open. Tammany does not expect that her opportunities are going to be prolonged indefinitely. When the explosion comes, it will be found that those who have been most deeply implicated have made arrangements by which they can conveniently run to cover. If citizens would tell all they know, short work could be made of it. Their hearts are brave, but their property interests are cowardly.

"There are parts of the town where young rowdies terrorize the street. The policeman says to you: 'I can't catch them.' It is an impressive sight to see policemen march on Decoration Day; but, after all, the most impressive thing they can do is to make crime dangerous. I can tell you where you can stand at certain hours of the day and see trained boys empty the pockets of the unwary. You need not go to Dickens in order to find a Fagin. Crime is not considered crime in this town unless it declines to be assessed, and the consequence is that young criminals are growing up among us, rank and thrifty. We have not studied this thing for the last eighteen months for nothing. Still we have no fear for the future. How long it will take to get there depends upon how many men there are that are willing to invest themselves and their names in the work of rendering present conditions disreputable, and therefore impossible."

The letters addressed to the Mayor, Superintendent Byrnes, and to Captain Devery were of a formal character, quoting from the Consolidation Act the duties and the powers of the police force, and specifying by street and number the resorts complained of in the Eleventh Precinct.

The letter to President Martin of the Board of Police Commissioners was as follows :

" The Board of Commissioners constitutes the determining power of the Police Department. It is upon you and your colleagues, therefore, that in the last analysis responsibility for the non-enforcement of law must always be conceded to rest. In view of this fact, we hereby transmit to you copies of communications which have to-day been sent to Thomas F. Gilroy, Mayor ; to Thomas Byrnes, Superintendent of the force ; and to William S. Devery, Captain of the Eleventh Precinct, calling upon you to exercise your proper authority in the matter, and to exert upon the force the pressure needed to secure the reasonable action asked for by the undersigned.

" The obligations of the Department are authoritatively and explicitly stated. While no one is so sanguine as to expect the complete rooting out of the gambling or of the social evil, we none of us have a right to expect that these evils will be played with by the Department. The law makes it your distinct duty to utilize the Department's power in repressing and preventing crime. No option is accorded you as to what classes of crime you shall repress and what not. The Department is executive, not legislative. The propriety of existing statutes relative to gambling and disorderly houses you may, as men, have an opinion upon, but not as commissioners. Your function is to act, not to philosophize. In the matter of action, it becomes immediately evident from the list of gambling-houses and houses of ill-fame herewith furnished that either you or your subordinates have been delinquent.

"The opinion has become current that such inaction is due to mercenary motives. The presentment of the March Grand Jury of 1892 indicated as much. However that may be, the suspicion that such charge is a valid one will not be eradicated from the public mind till the obligations devolving upon the Department are met with earnestness and thoroughness, of which the accompanying voluminous schedule gives not the slightest intimation. We expect, therefore, that you will give this matter your early attention, and that you will apply the force requisite to the closing of the places of which you are hereby notified."

## CHAPTER XVI

#### DENUNCIATION AND WHITEWASH

HAD we not understood quite well the animus of our police officers and commissioners, we should have been surprised at the evident irritation produced by our letters complaining of the condition of things in the Eleventh Precinct. If they had had a tithe of the anxiety to enforce the law which they professed to have, Martin, Sheehan, McClave, Byrnes, Williams, and Devery would have come up to our office on Twenty-second Street, to thank us with mellow and overflowing hearts for the valuable and detailed bits of criminal information which we had gratuitously furnished them. Notwithstanding all the efforts we have made during the past three years to help the Police Department earn its annual salary of $5,000,000, I do not recall a single instance in which an inexpensive return of thanks has been made to us by a police officer, or a cheap resolution of confidence in us voted by the Board of Police Commissioners.

The Commissioners met on the 17th of August, and Major Kipp was about to read our communication, when Mr. McClave inquired whether anything was to be gained by reading a letter that had appeared in the newspapers. "Certainly not," said President Martin. "I think," rejoined McClave, "that it is not worth while to waste time in reading it; I move that it be referred to the Superintendent for consideration and report."

The letter so referred was reported upon at the Board meeting one week later, at which time the official statement was received, accepted, and filed; but although the Superintendent, the Inspector, Captain, and a number of patrolmen in citizen's clothes had been scouring the Eleventh Precinct, each with a certified copy of our letters in his hand, nothing criminal had been observed, no iniquitous suggestion that put even a hypothetical stain on the monotonous whiteness of that immaculate district. If they had had the good sense to own up to *something*, even if it were nothing worse than the detection of a couple of ragamuffins pitching pennies, there would have been a semblance of probability about their report that would have relieved it; but the idea that the high functionaries of the New York Police were unable to get upon the trace or even presentiments of depravity in Delancey, Chrystie, and Bayard Streets, was too much even for the more gullible element of our community, and the elaborate whitewashing which the officials put upon each other was publicly accepted with mingled amusement and contempt.

In the meantime our office kept watch on that little

spot of municipal paradise, and knew how soon after our letters were issued Devery's crime factories closed up, and how soon they resumed again. Our men, however, for the following month, devoted the larger part of their energies to another field, and Devery, Williams, and Byrnes were allowed space for meditation and opportunity to repent and to bring forth fruits meet for repentance.

Having waited what seemed to us ample time for the development of a penitential mood, and discovering in that portion of town no symptoms of a change of spirit or of purpose, we brought our men again upon the same ground and, taking our former list again, made solid cases against most of the same houses *de novo*, forty-five in number. When this work had been completed in a way fully to satisfy the requirements of the legal members of our Executive Committee (Messrs. Frank Moss and T. D. Kenneson), another series of complaints was prepared and addressed to the same parties as before. This was on the 12th of October. The communication, transmitted to J. J. Martin, President of the Board of Police Commissioners, was as follows:

"Whatever may be the incapacity or duplicity of the agencies through which you aim to secure the enforcement of law, you will be obliged to concede that the responsibility for the condition of this city, in that particular, still rests with yourself and your colleagues; and at the expense of seeming to you repetitious, we take this means of informing you that the police precinct which you have placed in charge of Captain William S. Devery, and of which, for considerations doubtless appreciated by yourself, you are still retaining him in charge, is being administered by him in the same manner of incompetency, or of criminality—according as you may prefer to designate it—as that to which your attention was recently called by a letter emanating from the Society for the Prevention of Crime, and received by you August 10th. In our correspondence at that time we cited the statutes bearing upon the case, and we are pleased to see that neither the Mayor, your own Board, the Acting Superintendent of Police, the Inspecter nor the Captain of the Eleventh Precinct has taken any exception to the interpretation which those statutes were recognized by us as designed to carry. It appears, therefore, that the law in the premises we all interpret alike. The obligation of your department to proceed without dallying or subterfuge to the inspection of all suspected places, and to the repression and restraint of all unlawful places, is mutually conceded. There being no dispute, then, in the matter of law, the question resolves itself exclusively into one of fact.

"Here also we are clear in the ground which we occupy, and do not propose to be 'bluffed' by any system of mutual exculpation or raw denial with which the agencies of your Department rush to one another's relief. After the easy disposition which was made of our complaint received in August, we deemed it due to yourselves to afford ample time for the adoption of a policy more consistent with the responsibilities devolving upon you, but have diligently employed the interim in studying the habits of your Department with particular reference to the precinct in question. The spasm of zeal exhibited by your subordinates on the appearance of our complaint has never, for a day, deluded the gamblers or the bawdy-house keepers of the precinct into the supposition that their business was imperilled. However you may see fit to explain it, the criminals in that precinct expect more from the protection of your Department than fear from its inflictions. As already said, we have kept in touch with the precinct, and we desire to communicate to you herewith the results of our latest canvass, completed on October 4th. We knew in August, as we know now, that the reports made to your Board by Acting Superintendent Conlin, by Inspector Alexander S. Williams, and by Captain William S. Devery, whether by intention or otherwise, are misrepresentations of the truth in essential particulars; and however stinted may have been the hospitality which you evinced toward our complaint as then presented, you will now certainly, unless bound to others by ties as degrading as they would be unlawful, give to our renewed complaint a heed more in keeping with the dignity of your position and the gravity of the accusation.

"In a communication received by you in August last, the undersigned brought to your attention some fifty places at which gambling was being carried on, or which were being maintained as disorderly houses. Your response to the same, as made to your superior officer, has been forwarded to us. We know very well the ground on which we stand, and do not reopen the correspondence for any purpose of debating the matter with you. We have adopted our own scheme of action, and the notice which we now serve upon you is the second step in the pursuance of that policy, so far as it concerns yourself. We submit, herewith, for your consideration and action, a list of disorderly houses which are now doing business in your precinct. You will perceive that this list is substantially identical with that furnished you in August. In your report to Inspector Williams you claim to have visited these houses. Whether you visited them or not, they were in operation prior to that date; they were in operation subsequent to that date, and they were all of them in full blast on October 4th.

"Consistently with the obligations imposed upon you by the statutes and 'Rules and Regulations' under which you are acting, and which were quoted to you in our previous communication, we demand of you that you address yourself to this business without subterfuge or evasion, and that you proceed to close and to keep closed the places used for lewd or obscene purposes."

From our other communications we select only that addressed to Captain William S. Devery, of the Eleventh Precinct, as follows:

"We submit, then, herewith a list of disorderly houses which are at present flourishing under the administration of Captain Devery—our object in collecting this evidence being to show, not what kind of women keep the houses, but what kind of a captain keeps the precinct. Both now and heretofore our contention has not been with the disorderly houses *per se*, but with Captain Devery, and men like him, who, having accepted positions of grave authority, are failing, either from incompetence or from criminal complicity, to meet their obligations.

"By comparing the accompanying list with the one furnished you in August, you will perceive their substantial identity. The houses were running before the time when your subordinates claim to have visited them; have been running since, and were in full operation on the evening of October 4th; and not only in operation, but conducting their business in a manner which made profligacy an open fact, the whole region pestilential, and youthful escape from the foul contagion a physical and moral impossibility. Any claim that Captain Devery is so disguising the social evil as to make vice difficult in his precinct is a lie from bottom up; and unless you compel him to the decent discharge of his functions in that particular, your own souls will have the burden to carry of the physical and moral pollution which free and exhibitive lust are bound to entail."

We had two or three objects in thus repeating our blows. In the first place, more soreness will be induced by striking one spot twice than in striking two spots once. Besides that, we wanted to convince Martin and Sheehan that we were not amenable to any game of bluff. There was a constant expectation on their part that we were going to be tired pretty soon, and there was great satisfaction afforded to us in deferring their hopes. There was also another purpose in this second assault upon Devery which will disclose itself as the story proceeds.

It was with a kind of earnest curiosity that we awaited the effect of our second discharge. We had the satisfaction of knowing that whatever the Commissioners and their subordinates did, they were certain to be put in an awkward predicament. They would be obliged either to incriminate themselves by retreating from the position they had taken in August, or they would be obliged to stultify themselves by continuing to maintain that position. But a criminal will always prefer to make himself foolish rather than to confess himself wicked, and our complaint was received by the Board with even chillier hospitality than had been accorded to it in August. The matter came up before the Police Board on October 20th. Superintendent Byrnes reported that he had instructed Inspector Williams and Captain Devery to make a thorough investigation into the charges preferred in our last communication, and, if they found the law violated, to arrest the offender and report the result. In addition, the Superintendent detailed two Central Office detectives, furnishing them with lists of the places complained of, and directing them to visit separately, and unknown to each other, the specified places at irregular hours of the day or night, and to report. In his report to the Superintendent, Inspector Williams says :

"I have given the communication from Dr. Parkhurst and its charges of alleged open immorality in the Eleventh Precinct, and of intimated criminality on the part of Captain Devery in permitting such places to exist, the closest possible attention and investigation. I find that these charges are without foundation. I will further state that the report made by Captain Devery last August on a similar communication was true, and that there was positively no misrepresentation of any kind in either of these reports. As to gambling in the Eleventh Precinct, there is none; and any person who says that gambling is carried on there tells a deliberate and malicious falsehood.

"The alleged disorderly houses in the precinct were visited by officers in citizen's clothes, under my direction, previous to October 4th, and since October 4th, up to date, and no violation of the law was found. On receipt of this communication I detailed officers from outside the Eleventh Precinct to visit at irregular hours these houses, and in no case could they gain admittance, or procure evidence that would tend to show that the law was in any way violated.

"I have also frequently visited the streets and passed the houses mentioned in the communication, and have failed to find any of the 'open profligacy' or 'foul contagion' from which the writers of this communication would make it appear that 'youthful escape' was a 'moral impossibility,' and any person who would make such a statement in the face of the actual condition of the precinct has no regard for truth or his moral obligations.

"In conclusion, it is admitted by the signers of the communication that it is a personal attack on Captain Devery and not against disorderly houses. And the false accusations therein contained would never have been made, had not Captain Devery caused the arrest and conviction of the Superintendent of the Society for the Suppression of Vice, for blackmail."

After the above reports had been read by Chief Clerk Kipp, they were accepted and filed. At this point Commissioner MacLean moved that the Inspector and Captain mentioned in our communication be given permission to bring action for libel against the signers of the paper. Commissioners Martin, McClave, and Sheehan declined to step into the hole which Mr. MacLean, with characteristic courtesy, had dug for them. Mr. Sheehan, who keeps in stock a good deal of righteous indignation of a certain sort, and who felt himself severely rubbed at the spot where that commodity is deposited, followed the defeat of Mr. MacLean's pleasant suggestion with the following remarks, quoted from the report in the *World* of the day following:

"Gentlemen," then said Mr. Sheehan, "I believe it will be conceded that since I have been a member of this board, I have always been inclined to favor Dr. Parkhurst in furnishing him and his Society with any documents or information that we might have which would be of service to his Society, for the reason that I thought he was honestly endeavoring to perform what he considered public duty. I find, however, that I have been entirely mistaken. Within the past few days I have read interviews given to the newspapers by Dr. Parkhurst, in which he says that he wished it to be distinctly understood that he and his assistants were not fighting disorderly houses, saloons, and gambling-houses, but that they were fighting Tammany Hall. The public had been led to believe otherwise. The people supposed that the one object and end of Dr. Parkhurst and his Society was war on saloons and disorderly houses.

" Has the reverend gentleman's vocation departed, or is he only coming out now under his true colors? It seems to me," concluded the Commissioner, "that henceforth no attention whatever should be paid by this Board to any communications from Dr. Parkhurst or his Society. His harangues shall receive only the same attention as is given to other Republican stump speakers who are continually howling for the destruction of the Democratic party."

The thorough and wicked insincerity of the Commissioners will be understood from the following paragraph of an interview had with us on the day following:

" Our complaints of August and October made Byrnes, Williams, and Devery defendants in the case. They are the parties whose guilt or innocence it was incumbent upon the Commissioners to demonstrate. Instead of investigating the matter themselves, the Commissioners have delegated the duty to the very defendants whose alleged incompetence or criminality we insisted on being examined into. They have said to the accused : ' You may retire, decide what you think of yourselves and each other, and bring in a verdict.' The verdict came in yesterday, whereupon the astute Commissioners turn to the waiting public and say, 'Non proven.' Whether that means that the Commissioners believe their subordinates to be so innocent that it would be an insult to them to have them investigated, or so criminal that it would be awkward for the Commissioners themselves, we have no present opinion that we care to express. But considered as a purely judicial process, it is a mixture of farce and tragedy that touches some of us at the spot where we keep our unutterable loathing. If we supposed that the object of the Commissioners was not to clear the culprits but to get at the bottom facts, we think we could put them in reach of a few such facts. They need our help a great deal more than we need theirs. Sheehan, with an inflection that is tenderly tinged with pathos, is reported as saying at the meeting yesterday that we had not shown a disposition to avail of his support. We don't want his support. We are not sailing in his boat. If he wants to sail in our boat a little while, perhaps we might conclude to take him aboard and cruise around with him, touching at occasional points within the jurisdiction of his Department, where he could pick up a pertinent fact or two, that would enable him and his colleagues to bring in a verdict of their own, and not simply a verdict that had been put in their mouths by their suspected subordinates." At the very moment when the whitewashing process was going on at the Police Commissioners' room yesterday afternoon, an arrest was made at a house in Forsyth Street, named in Captain Devery's report as having been closed October 4th, but when visited by our detectives on Tuesday and Thursday of this week was found to be running as usual. We obtained a warrant from Justice Voorhis, and the keeper of the house spent the night in the Essex Market jail."

All these events were doing their steady work in the opinions and feelings of the community. *We* were being defeated at every turn, but the *cause* we represented was winning. It was becoming increasingly evident to men with an intelligence and a conscience, that unrighteousness was so pervasively wrought into the structure of our city government, that honesty and decency had no rights which it felt itself bound to respect, and that evil was so deeply intrenched that nothing short of a revolution would avail to shatter and subvert it. Thus, while the movement of our cause was outwardly retrograde, it was substantially onward and forward.

# CHAPTER XVII

### THE BROOME STREET MOB

It is important that there be a clear understanding of the point at which we are now arrived. We had ample proof of the existence of more than sixty gambling and disorderly places in the Eleventh Precinct. We told the Police Department we had such proof, and they told us we lied, or words to that effect. That was in August. In October we secured fresh proof against forty places of the same character in the same precinct, and for the most part identical with those complained of in August. We told the department we had such proof and again they told us we lied, only this time with a sneer. We were, however, on a sure trail, and had no intention of being browbeaten. With so much accomplished, and accomplished to our own satisfaction and to that of the town, there was only one thing that remained to do next, and that was to select a certain number of Devery's pest-holes, that Devery, Williams, Byrnes and the commissioners had given the public to understand had no existence outside of our incompetent and vicious imaginations, gather fresh evidence upon them, and take them before the Grand Jury as ground for Devery's indictment.

This was easily done. Even granting that Byrnes and his associates had been conscientiously unable to discover criminal conduct in the resorts we complained of, they could easily have prevented the continuance of such conduct if they had chosen to. There was, however, no such effort made on their part, because there was no such desire. The forty resorts were soon in the full swing of their criminal industries again, and we had no difficulty in securing against them all the evidence required.

We selected four houses from the number of those that had been specified in both our previous complaints, and made against them cases so strong that nothing which made pretence to justice or legality could suffice to break them.

These cases were tried at the Court of Special Sessions on the 14th of November, before Justices Grady, Smith, and McMahon.

The judicial lights just specified were not altogether of such quality as to thrill us with ardent anticipation, but at any rate we knew our cases were well made, and besides that, there was one influence operating that was decidedly in our favor. The November election of '93 had been held the week before, and there was an exceptional amount of moral ozone in the air. Brooklyn had just broken its municipal ring, and the cause of honest government was looking up.

People were beginning to recover the courage of their convictions. Decency was coming to mean more. There was an amount of moral pressure beginning to exert itself that even Tammany Justices felt themselves beholden to reckon with.

We can argue against the propriety of public sentiment affecting judicial procedure, but it does affect it all the same. It will, to a degree, vitiate the findings of honest judges and jurors, and it will to a degree rectify the findings of dishonest judges and jurors. Whatever theory we may hold upon the question abstractly, there was sentiment in the atmosphere, that 14th of November, that had not been there two weeks before, and it contributed incalculably to the issues of the day. The testimony of our witnesses was strong and lucid, and the prosecution was ably conducted by Messrs. Moss and Kenneson of our Executive Committee. The verdict of guilty was promptly rendered in each of the four cases, and sentence pronounced.

We have been thus explicit in our recital of this matter for the reason that the convictions secured that day constituted a crisis in the history of our work; and a crisis, too, that was scarcely appreciated by the judicial gentlemen who sat upon the Bench. We had been a year and a half in reaching that point, and the decisions rendered in our favor by the Court was the proof upon which was to hang everything coming after. The simple fact was, that three Tammany Justices had been compelled by the indubitable evidence which we furnished, to render a verdict that practically convicted Divver, Martin, Byrnes, and the Police Commissioners, either of absolute ignorance of matters with which they ought to have been thoroughly acquainted, or of secret sympathy with a condition of things which ought to have excited their official indignation and moral disgust.

Before going on, now, to speak of the use which we made of the convictions thus secured, it will be necessary to go back a couple of weeks and describe the brutal handling of our detectives by the "Broome Street Mob," on the afternoon of October 27th, at the same hour, significantly enough, when the Police Commissioners in their office on Mulberry Street, were considering our last complaint touching the Eleventh Precinct, and whitewashing the captain (Devery) in whose precinct the mobbing outrage was committed. The coincidence might almost be considered as a providential rap at the humbuggery of the Police Commissioners who did the whitewashing, and at the false testimony of the superior police officials upon which the finding of the Commissioners was based. The report of this event which, almost more than any other, has evidenced the animosity cherished toward us by the Superintendent of Police, his immediate subordinates and the thugs who stood in with them, can best be related in the words of John H. Lemmon, who is a tried and faithful member of our detective force, and who, as the reader will see, was himself personally participant in the scenes which he describes:

"On Friday afternoon, October 27th, accompanied by four other detectives of the Society, we appeared before Justice Voorhis to prosecute three of the women who it has just been said were tried and convicted November 14th. It having been noised around the precinct that these women would be arraigned, numbers of their friends, including hangers-on, blacklegs, thugs, Tammany heelers and other friends of the keepers of disorderly houses in the precinct, made their way to Essex Market Police Court. Their appearance was such that the Court Officers drove them from the entrance. They, however, lingered about on the street adjacent to the Court, waiting for us to come out.

"A little after four o'clock, Messrs. Moss and Kenneson, of our Executive Committee, left the courtroom, and being unknown to the crowd were not recognized as being connected with the case. They, however, did not like the looks of the crowd, and taking a stand on the opposite side of the street, watched developments. We had learned of the presence of the crowd outside, and that their numbers were being constantly augmented. Mr. Moss returned and told us that we had better separate, each of us going our own way. We objected to this, knowing full well that our safety depended on our remaining together. As we came out we found fully one hundred and fifty men, and they at once closed around us. One who was in advance of the crowd sprang toward me with a knife in his hand, which was drawn back ready to strike. (I have since learned this man's name and address.) One of our detectives exclaimed 'Look out, Lemmon, he is going to knife you.' I at once jumped away and faced my assailant, and saw him, knife in hand, being hustled away by some of his crowd. We walked on, hoping the crowd would disperse, as none of us was prepared for a row. But the crowd continued to increase. The mob followed closely upon us, growing in size, their numbers being added to by loungers and others from the various saloons and other such places as we passed along. As they would meet a crowd they would remark 'We are after the Parkhurst men, and are going to do them up.' These threats were heard by a number of responsible parties, including Messrs. Moss and Kenneson who, not being recognized, walked along in the crowd without fear of being molested.

"When we arrived at the corner of Allen Street, we met a policeman on duty, and one of our men went up to him and said: 'I call upon you to disperse this mob, or we shall have a man killed here.' The policeman laughed at us, and paid no attention to the request. We paused only for a moment, as by this time the crowd had grown to fully five hundred people, and they were pressing us pretty closely. The crowd was not the usual howling mob, which expends most of its energy in wind, but had a decidedly business air about it.

"When we reached the Bowery, I suggested that we take a Fourth Avenue car, thinking it possible the crowd would follow us no farther. One had just passed and we had to wait. We crossed over the street, the mob still at our heels, and growing bolder every minute. A car was coming, and it seemed only a question of seconds whether we should be assaulted or not. Just as the car came up we attempted to board it, but I was cut off by a passing beer-wagon and separated from the others. I made a dash around it and jumped on the front of the car. A man leaped on the other side and struck at me. I dodged the blow and struck my assailant, which knocked him off the car. At the same time the crowd surged around the car, two men grabbing the bridles of the horses and stopping them.

"In the meantime the other four men were near the rear of the car, trying to board it. A big, burly-looking ruffian gave one of our men a stinging blow on the cheek. Others of the mob struck at our men while boarding the car, but they succeeded in avoiding the ruffians.

"We finally made our way into the car, in which there were a number of passengers, who were badly frightened. Numbers of the mob jumped on the car at both ends, and tried to force their way inside; but our men stood at the doors, and, assisted by the conductor, who was very roughly handled, kept them back. Two policemen, who were attracted by the crowd, rushed to the rescue of the Society's officers, and pulled their assailants from the car. To the credit of these two policemen, I want to say they worked manfully, so far as I could see, and by their well-directed energy discouraged the rioters. As soon as the men holding the horses released them, the driver plied his whip with a will, and we went up the street at a full run, leaving a crowd of fully fifteen hundred men, which had collected during the row at the car.

"In the meantime, I was having a very exciting experience. The pressure was so great on the front of the car, that, being separated from my friends, I left it and boarded a Third Avenue car, when I was again attacked by some of the mob who had noticed my movements. I, however, succeeded in again knocking off my assailant, but things became so warm I had to make another change, and bolted for a Fourth Avenue car which happened to be passing, but was followed by my pursuers. I was once more attacked, but was fortunate enough to push my assailant off the car, and immediately left from the other side and made my way to the Grand Street station of the Elevated road. Two men followed me and took the same car. When the train arrived at Twenty-third Street, I turned to them and threatened to make them trouble if they attempted to follow me farther. They evidently thought they had had enough, and concluded to give up further pursuit. I then went to the office of the Society and reported. Afterward I went to Dr. Parkhurst's house and informed him of what had happened."

Exasperating as this mobbing affray in some respects was, it was highly interesting as an object-lesson of the fact that when we pushed the Superintendent and Inspector and the Captain beyond a certain point, the thugs flew to their relief, showing by incontestable proof that they knew who their friends were. Nothing, perhaps, has occurred in the history of our dealings with the high police officials that has been to them a more fruitful source of mortification, or that has made more friends for our cause, especially in the lower parts of the town. The Superintendent had plumed himself upon the fact that however much hidden crime there might be in the city, anybody could walk the streets, in daylight at least, without fear of molestation. This event on Broome Street gave the lie to his brag. We were curious to know what he would do about it. Our Executive Committee immediately decided that we should ourselves take no action. We had laid repeated complaints before the administrative and executive heads of the department without effect, and concluded that we could fish with more effect in other waters.

Mr. Byrnes sent to me for our detectives, and I returned word to him that they were at his service. Mr. Moss called at the Superintendent's office, and in describing his visit there, says: "I saw Mr. Byrnes, and he said he knew who committed the outrage, and damned them roundly, and said that he would sift the matter to the bottom, and would have the guilty parties, no matter who they were or how high they were. He said it was a bad condition of affairs if a mob could drive our men half a mile through the streets without interference, and the honor of the Police Department was at stake. He was earnest and profane."

Three of the ringleaders were arrested by Byrnes. Mr. Lemmon further testified as follows:

"These three arrested parties were all identified by our detectives at Police Headquarters, among them the one who had attempted to assassinate me. I was sent for by Superintendent Byrnes and requested to appear at Essex Market Court for the purpose of identifying, if I could, any of the men whom he had arrested on information furnished him by us. I accordingly went to Essex Market Court, and there heard the keeper instructed to 'line-up' ten men in the jail and take me in and see if I could identify any of those who had figured in the mob. I waited for about thirty minutes, and finally was told by Captain Devery that they were ready. I went into the jail, which was a dark, dingy place, and in the very darkest part of the jail I saw about twenty men, all in a line, with their backs turned to the light, making it as hard for me to identify them as possible. I went up and down the line several times, while Captain Devery and the other officials stood and watched me. I finally turned to Devery and his men and told him that I had picked out two of the people whom I would swear were in the mob, one of whom, I stated, was the man who had attempted to assassinate me. I was told to go back and place my hand on the men whom I could identify. I accordingly did this, and placed my hand on Sugar, and remarked, 'This is the man that stabbed at me; I will swear to it. This other man was in the mob, and one of the ringleaders on the Bowery.' After I had done this, Captain Devery had the impudence to say to me, ' Who gave you the pointers so as to identify these men?' I informed him that I did not have any pointers as to how to identify these men, nor did I need any pointers of him or anyone else. After this was done, three prisoners, two of whom I had identified and three of whom all the other detectives had personally identified, were taken into the court and arraigned before the judge. I was asked if I positively identified the man who had stabbed at me, and I told him that I had, and pointed him out."

It is unnecessary to rehearse all the efforts made by the Superintendent to get out of the hole into which he had placed himself by the voluble profanity by which he had committed himself to the cause of justice while in conference with Mr. Moss. He insisted that we should assume the part of prosecutors. We refused, and told him to mind what was his own business and not ours, and do the prosecuting himself. We were informed that if we did not prosecute, the prisoners would be discharged. We said, "Discharge them then. If the Superintendent of Police does not care enough for the duties of his office and the reputation of his Department to prosecute a lot of vagabonds who, in broad daylight, have set upon the agents of a chartered society quietly engaged in doing what, as such agents, it belonged to them to do, let him stand by the record of his criminal neglect, and bear the ignominy of it."

The prisoners were discharged on November 3d. The Superintendent decided that there had been no mob! By no means, probably, could the Superintendent have made more distinctly apparent his total unsympathy with the cause of clean and honest municipal administration for which our Society inflexibly stands.

## CHAPTER XVIII

#### WAR ON THE CAPTAINS

THE chapter just concluded is parenthetical and deals only with an incident that branched off from the main line of events. We have now to recur to the point at which we had arrived upon securing our four convictions in the Court of Special Sessions, November 13th.

These convictions were against the keepers of four disorderly houses in Devery's precinct, of which complaint had been made in our letter addressed to the Department both in August and October. The Commissioners, on the testimony of Byrnes, Williams and Devery, had declared in both of those months that there were no such places in the precinct. We therefore showed the whitewashing character of their report, and the falsity of the testimony upon which it was based, by taking the keepers of four houses specified in both complaints, having them arrested, tried, convicted, and sentenced.

With this material in hand we went before the Grand Jury and secured four indictments against Captain Devery on the 29th of November. The indictment of a captain was a great event, not to say an unprecedented one. It was a little like the thinning of the clouds after a long storm, which still leaves it probable that there may yet be a good deal more rain, but suggests that there are new influences creeping into the atmosphere and that it is not going to rain always. The feeling of the community was well expressed by the following editorial paragraphs taken from the *Morning Advertiser* on the following day :

"The victory achieved by the Rev. Dr. Parkhurst in securing the indictment of Captain Devery for misdemeanor in permitting the existence of disorderly houses in his precinct, is not only encouraging to the decent people who are striving to clean out the moral plague spots which are corrupting the municipality itself, but it is significant of the fact the public begins to feel and understand, that despite the power and strength of Tammany Hall, the people are even more powerful, when aroused, and the machinery of the law can be successfully invoked to work the reforms to which they are devoted.

"A few months ago there was a feeling that the conspiracy headed by Mr. Croker was all-powerful for evil, and that it was scarcely worth while to struggle against it; and it was a question whether this indictment could have been secured so long as jurors were given to understand that Tammany would 'get even' with the man who attacked any of its minions.

"It may also be taken by these heelers as a warning that they may, after all, reach the end of their ropes in time. Neither the boss nor the organization itself is always able to protect them, as they have always believed. The people have some rights and there is law to secure them, and that law can be made operative."

These indictments offered us a certain amount of promise, and yet promise that in our collected moments we never expected to see fulfilled. If it had been possible to disassociate Devery from the Police Department, we felt that it would have been easy to convict him. He was not attending to his duties in the Eleventh Precinct; community was satisfied of that, and the Grand Jury were convinced of it, and it was not difficult to persuade an intelligent jury of the fact. The trouble, however, was that in convicting him they would be convicting not him only, but the whole of the Police Department, for they were all in it, and were all committed to it. That is why we were gratified by the indictment of Devery without being in the least degree elated by it.

Devery was not brought to trial until the following April, and was acquitted. The large attendance of police captains indicated that they realized that it was their trial as much as it was his. The Superintendent committed himself to the support of the defendant to the extent of indicating his confidence in the reports upon the condition of the precinct made to him by his detectives, and upon which had been based his own exculpating report to the Commissioners. One of the effects of the way in which the prosecution was conducted by Assistant District-Attorney Weeks, was to make us long more ardently for the time when the District-Attorney's office should become in this city a stronghold of justice, to the dismay of the criminal and the encouragement of the righteous.

Captain Devery's acquittal was distinctly a victory for the Police Department and the other vicious elements of the community, but even for them the victory was an expensive one, for the time had now arrived when success gained by our enemy ceased to secure the applause of the people at large, or to check the rising and strengthening current of popular indignation. Devery's acquittal, in view of the strength of the case we had against him, was a boon to our cause for which we shall never cease to be profoundly grateful.

A month after the indictment had been found, we undertook, on the 27th day of December, to secure an indictment against Inspector Williams and Captain Schmittberger. Devery's precinct lay within Williams's inspection district; and if the Grand Jury considered Devery delinquent as captain, for having a filthy precinct, it seemed reasonable to expect (and the opinion subsequently stated by Judge Barrett justified our expectation) that it would consider Williams delinquent as an inspector for having to that extent a filthy inspection district. Unfortunately, however, we had now a different Grand Jury to deal with. There were sitting in December both the regular jury and an Extraordinary one. We desired to bring Williams and Schmittberger before the former, but for some reason the District-Attorney was concerned to have the regular jury discharged, notwithstanding the fact that its members had expressed themselves as willing to sit longer if the Society for the Prevention of Crime had any cases to bring before them. It is not easy to explain Nicoll's anxiety to get them out of the way, unless we attribute it to his acquaintance with the fact that they were desirous of handling our interests and gave token of possessing the intelligence and integrity to handle them with. And so we were shoved off onto the Extraordinary Jury—against which we had been earnestly warned—and suffered defeat.

We are not whining, but we desire that there should be a clear and widespread understanding of the solid wall of opposition against which all our blows had to be delivered. The District-Attorney's office has been, from the first, an obdurate obstacle and a biting exasperation. It was well-nigh impossible to gain entrance to the Grand-Jury room, except over the recalcitrant and protesting body of the District-Attorney. In the matter of Schmittberger, just referred to, the mutual antipathy of the District-Attorney's office and our own reached its climax. After our charge against Williams and Schmittberger had been thrown out by the Extraordinary Jury, I issued, in behalf of the Society for the Prevention of Crime, a statement covering the previous six months of our controversy with the District-Attorney, which is too long to be inserted entire, but which was excellently summarized at the time by Dr. J. N. Hallock (editor of the *Christian at Work*, a member of the Society for the Prevention of Crime), and printed in his issue of January 11, 1894, as follows :

"Dr. Parkhurst's two strong points are a thorough conviction of the righteousness of his cause and his entire confidence in the intelligence and moral sense of the people. And in no instance are these more conspicuous than in the appeal he has just made from the District-Attorney's office in this city directly to the people in the case of Inspector Williams and Captain Schmittberger, who are charged with a plain and wilful neglect of their duty. Such an appeal he has shown to be not only wise, but absolutely necessary. All the influence which is possessed by the combination of politics and crime that governs New York has been exerted to prove that the work of Dr. Parkhurst is based upon a misconception of the law and of the facts, and that therefore his charges really have no standing in court. The failure of the Grand Jury to indict Schmittberger and Williams would, of course, be paraded as actual proof of the unsubstantial nature of his work. The statement of Dr. Parkhurst puts the responsibility for the failure where it belongs, and New York and her perplexed and outraged friends, as well as the better classes of the people everywhere, are delighted to have found at last a man and a Society who dare and are able to persist in fighting for the enforcement of law and the removal from power of the partners in crime, with as great pertinacity as those who violated the law. Dr. Parkhurst has vividly and tersely given the story of the efforts of the Society to secure indictments, and has placed ex-District-Attorney Nicoll right where he belongs, and at the same time effectively notified Colonel Fellows that the men behind the organization know the law, and are not to be bulldozed or cowed into inaction. He reviews the history of the Society's dealings with the District-Attorney's office and the Grand Jury for the past six months. The public is familiar with the greater part of it, but there is one incident to which attention should be called. After unsuccessful efforts to induce Mr. Nicoll to present the evidence against the police captains to the Grand Jury last summer, a meeting was arranged by the District-Attorney and Mr. Cross, the foreman of the jury, and Mr. Frank Moss, the lawyer of the Society. The men were brought together by Mr. Nicoll, and both he and Mr. Cross argued that no attack should be made upon the police at that time, because there might be labor riots in September. Mr. Moss thought on that very account the police should be looked after at once, so that they would know what was required of them and be in condition to work if the possible riots appeared. But no evidence collected by the Society could be got before that jury. Mr. Cross was again foreman in December, and when the evidence was at last submitted he failed to find indictments. When the November jury indicted Captain Devery, Dr. Parkhurst was refused the jury-room till he had agreed not to ask for the indictment of Superintendent Byrnes. Efforts were made to get before the regular December jury, and they were also anxious to hear from the Society. But Dr. Parkhurst was put off until it was too late to summon witnesses, although he was told that he might present his case on the last day of the term. He could not get ready on such short notice, and finally, after he had informed the public of this treatment, arrangements were made to allow him to appear before the Extraordinary Jury, of which Mr. Cross, the man who had urged Mr. Moss not to attack the police, was foreman. This last statement shows why indictments were not found, and makes evident the fact that vital evidence was purposely omitted by the District-Attorney. Every man of average intelligence knows that Williams and Schmittberger could not possibly be ignorant of the existence of houses of ill-repute which they had not closed, and no one believes that an impartial jury would have failed to indict these men if the facts could have been given, as they would have been given, if the District-Attorney had not interfered. It was evidently without a knowledge of these facts that some of the Grand Jury innocently recommended that there be harmony and concerted action between the Police Department and the Society for the Prevention of Crime. . . .

"In conclusion, Dr. Parkhurst writes these ringing and truthful words — words which will live long after Tammany has been overthrown and ceased to exist even in the memory of New Yorkers: 'Justice will not be a common commodity in this city until the District-Attorney's office is held by one whose judicial sense is not mortgaged to his political affiliations, and whose loyalty to his friends does not interfere with his sworn obligation to mete out to all classes their independent and impartial dues. This statement will have served its purpose if it shall have made somewhat more evident to the community the stress of wind and tide against which we have to make head, and the impossibility of securing in this city anything more than the caricature of justice, till at the polls some of the joints and ligaments have been broken that knit our municipal government into a compact body of brigandage and defiance.'"

Whatever might be the immediate issue of such efforts, the Society still felt that the best means of strengthening the growing sentiment of community would be to continue in the same line of warfare upon other captains whose precincts were exceptionally corrupt, and we selected as the next candidate for our attention, Captain Richard Doherty, then of the Fourteenth Precinct. All of this seems small matter now, at a time when one captain is behind bars and so many are being measured for their striped suits; but it was all we could do at the time, and fulfilled its object by paving the way for results of a more pronounced character to be achieved by the Senate Committee further on. Later, in November of '93, we had made a careful examination of Captain Doherty's precinct, and had completed thirty-five cases of gambling and disorderly houses, and sent the letters to Doherty, to the Superintendent, and the Commissioners, and demanded that the police do their duty and close the places up.

A more important move was that made against Captain Slevin, of the Oak Street Station. Near the end of December, in the same year, in our letter of complaint, gambling and disorderly houses were specified by street and number, and we were prepared, if necessary, to back up our charges by evidence that had been carefully secured. The letter which we addressed to the Commissioners was as follows :

" *To the Honorable the Board of Police Commissioners.*"

"GENTLEMEN : We submit to you herewith copies of communications which have this day been transmitted to Thomas Byrnes, Superintendent of Police, and to Captain Edward Slevin, of the Fourth Police Precinct.

" While not members of the Police Department, you nevertheless constitute its administrative head, and are, in the last analysis, responsible for everything in the way of either incompetency, negligence, or criminality that distinguishes any part of the service.

" It is incumbent upon us, therefore, to direct your attention to the subjoined list of resorts which have been found by our detectives to be maintained as disorderly houses, and to demand that you immediately see to it that the pressure of the Department is exercised in the immediate and impartial suppression of the same.

" By examining the files in your office you will discover that complaints for the non-enforcement of law have been, on three occasions, urged by the Society for the Prevention of Crime against this same officer.

" Your own appreciation of the fitness of things, it

would seem, would hardly make it necessary for us to say that in order to determine fully the validity of our complaint, you will need to employ agencies other than those which are by the terms of the complaint made defendants in the case.

     " Respectfully yours,
       " C. H. PARKHURST,
       " T. D. KENNESON,
       " FRANK MOSS,
         *Executive Committee.*

"December 22, 1893."

The following paragraph appeared in our address to Captain Slevin :

"Your official position presupposes your acquaintance with the statute and the rule above cited, and it would be superfluous to bring them to your notice were it not that their intent is evidently missed or ignored by you in your administration of the affairs of your own precinct.

" We ask no question as to the reasons for your disregard of the specific requirements just quoted. We simply affirm the fact of such disregard, and insist upon it that you correct your methods of administration. In particular we demand that you at once deal in the manner prescribed with the following places situated in your precinct, which our detectives have repeatedly visited, and which they are prepared to show are being run as disorderly houses."

The report made to the Commissioners by Byrnes, on January 5th following, exonerated Slevin, but the

Commissioners deferred action until further information should be obtained from the Excise Board. When this information was received, early in February following, it confirmed the truth of our charges, and put in an awkward position Inspector Williams, Superintendent Byrnes, and Captain Slevin, who had agreed in presenting a whitewashing report to the Commissioners. It was then that the Commissioners asked our Society to furnish them the evidence which we had obtained against the houses complained of in Slevin's precinct. This we declined to do, and replied to them in the following letter, which is reproduced in full, as exhibiting with some completeness the general situation at that date.

" *To the Honorable the Police Commissioners:*
" Your request has been considered carefully and respectfully, and we regret to feel ourselves obliged to decline the same, and for the following reasons :
" 1. Being yourselves an integral part of the Department whose fidelity our Society has made it a part of its business to impeach, you are an interested party, and therefore naturally lack that quality of impartiality which can alone fit you to sit in judgment upon adduced testimony, or make your finding to be of judicial value.
" 2. We have a number of times approached you with information carefully prepared and honestly intended, but the indifference, and, in one instance, contempt, with which such information was received by you affords us no ground upon which to suppose that

any additional facts upon the same lines would be regarded any more seriously by you were we to put them before you.

"3. The character of the testimony adduced before the Board of Excise by some of your own detectives against certain of the houses of which we have complained to you, leads us to feel that, if evidence as to the condition of things in the Fourth Precinct is what you want, you already have it. The charges to which they have sworn already go beyond anything which we have alleged in our complaint to you.

"4. Our reluctance to avail of your Board as a tribunal before which to seek the convictions of any officer of the force is greatly enhanced by the issue of all such efforts in the past. Four captains have been tried before your Board since 1887 on complaint of private citizens. First, Captain Alexander S. Williams was tried on charges signed by Howard Crosby and others. There were thirty-five witnesses for the prosecution. Commissioner Porter alone rendered an opinion, which was a scorching one, and thoroughly sustained the prosecution, and held that corrupt consideration was the ground of Williams's neglect. After a delay of six weeks the Board voted two to two. At the same session Williams was promoted to the position of inspector. Second, Captains Carpenter and McLaughlin were subsequently tried on specifications signed by D. J. Whitney and Howard Crosby. Commissioners voted two to two. The testimony had all been referred to Commissioner Voorhis, who reported to the Board that the charges were sustained. Shortly after McLaughlin was promoted to the position of inspector. Third, Subsequently to this, Captain Killilea was tried on complaint of the Forty-fourth Street Association. The result was the same, tie vote. Recently an inspector (Williams) and two captains were put on trial by Superintendent Byrnes for neglect of duty, and Commissioner Voorhis, having been succeeded by Mr. Sheehan, the vote for conviction was reduced to one, and that for acquittal increased to three.

" 5. We may add to this also the fact that we do not care to impair the value of our detectives by submitting them any oftener than is necessary to the scrutiny of your officers, to say nothing of the personal violence to which they would render themselves liable if, as in the instance of their appearance at the Essex Market Court, they were to adventure themselves in that part of the city unprotected."

So far as I am aware this case of Slevin has never been disposed of.

In January, 1894, we studied up Captain Price's bailiwick, from which more complaints had reached us than from almost any other. The steps taken by us were similar to those taken in the previous instances and need not be specified.

In April of 1894 we set our men at work on Captain Martens's Precinct (Station-house on East Thirty-fifth Street), and instead of issuing letters complaining of several resorts, concentrated our charges upon one house, and that in easy view of my own residence, and almost directly beneath the droppings of Martens's official sanctuary. The following letter was sent to him, signed, as in every case, by the three members of the Executive Committee:

"*To F. W. Martens, Captain of the Twenty-first Precinct.*

"Sir: Our object in this communication is to call your attention to the filthy resort which you are tolerating at Corcoran's Saloon, southwest corner of Third Avenue and Thirty-fifth Street. It would hardly seem necessary that your attention should be 'called' to the place, however, as it is situated close by you—almost under the shadow of your own station-house, in fact—so that information from us ought to be the last thing in the world that could be of service to you.

"There are but few resorts which our detectives have visited that are reported by them as being so open and unblushingly vile. Being less than thirty paces from the station-house, your officers, of course, are continually filing past it, and it would be an insult to your powers of discernment, as well as theirs, to imagine that you are ignorant of the matter, at least in its general features. Viciousness under its elegant disguises may have its apologists, but in the resort referred to there are no disguises about it. It is a den of frank, brute animalism, and you know it; of course you know it.

"We have been trying to conceive what sort of instincts you are animated by that you can enjoy or even endure the close proximity of a hole that is so ingeniously filthy. We have observed the like proximity in the instance of certain other station-houses. Perhaps you can tell us whether there is any special significance attaching to such proximity. We do not mean to imply that the Department considers such a resort a necessary adjunct of the official headquarters of a precinct; still any man is a fool that supposes that Corcoran can put a bawdy-house annex onto his saloon and run it up so close to your office without there being a certain amount of understanding between the two institutions.

"If, as we would fain believe, your instincts are outraged by the proximity of such a nest of nastiness, by what sedative considerations are we to suppose that those instincts are kept tranquil under the severe and constant aggravation? We merely want to know what counterweight you avail of to preserve the equanimity of your righteous soul when pulled upon by the distracting irritations of Corcoran's dive.

"It is an interesting feature of the case that although Commissioner MacLean was known to have taken steps last Friday looking to your investigation before the Board, your neighbor on the corner, and other neighbors only a little more remote, were running their lecherous traffic with the same openness and enthusiasm Friday evening that they had been in the earlier part of the week; all of which, at least, suggests the confidence you have in the bulk of the Commissioners.

"The Society for the Prevention of Crime has never claimed that the social evil is going to be entirely eradicated, but there are depths of sexual brutality that no man that has not become a beast can contemplate without revulsion and loathing, and an institution of that character you are tolerating, if not protecting, at the place specified.

"We make no apology for the unequivocal terms in which we have couched our complaint. We are dealing with a captain who has recently been convicted of shabby discharge of official duty, and there are times when language that is impassioned and indignant is the only mode of address which self-respecting men have either the power or the right to employ.

"Executive Committee,
"C. H. PARKHURST,
"T. D. KENNESON,
"FRANK MOSS.

"Rooms of the Society for the Prevention of Crime,
"United Charities Building. April 23, 1894."

# CHAPTER XIX

### THE CHAMBER OF COMMERCE APPEALS TO ALBANY

No event has transpired during the history of our work that has operated more directly and powerfully to define and compact popular sentiment than the acquittal of Captain Devery. It was far more to our advantage that we were defeated in our efforts against him than it would have been had we been successful. The public was satisfied with the proofs which we presented of his criminal negligence; and his acquittal under those circumstances was a telling demonstration of the fact that when it is a matter of trying a policeman, facts and proofs are of no significance. It convinced reputable people that we had reached a point here in this city where might makes right, and that the only move by which right could be restored to its proper supremacy was by puncturing our iniquitous system to its vitals, and effecting its complete subversion. We had expected the acquittal of Devery, and were serenely resigned to such issue, believing that our defeat, in this instance, so far from shaking the popular confidence in our cause, would rather knit it into tougher tension, and that the people would in some way soon voice themselves in a manner full of promise and effect. For some time there had been in the air the premonition of a popular demand for some kind of authoritative investigation of the Police Department that should be qualified to reach the innermost facts of the situation. The Society for the Prevention of Crime was scarcely disposed to move in the matter, especially as we were not persuaded that if a special tribunal were constituted, or a Committee of Investigation were sent down from Albany, it would be any improvement on previous experiments of the same kind. It is not an easy thing to find any considerable number of men, inured to political methods and saturated with political influences, that can be trusted to do thorough work along lines where political considerations are liable to present and assert themselves.

While the Society for the Prevention of Crime and the public at large were standing in this earnest but waiting posture, the effective initiative was taken by the Chamber of Commerce.

At a special meeting of that body, held on January 25, 1894, the following resolutions were presented and moved by Mr. Gustav H. Schwab:

"*Resolved*, That the Committee of Five,* appointed by the Chairman to represent this Chamber before the Legislature and the Constitutional Convention of this

---

* This Committee, which had just been appointed by the President of the Chamber, consisted of J. Edward Simmons, Samuel D. Babcock,

State, be requested to advocate the separation of municipal elections from the State and national elections, and genuine ballot reform.

"*Resolved*, That said Committee be further requested to advocate a single head for the Police Department of this city.

"*Resolved*, That, in the opinion of this Chamber, there should be a thorough legislative investigation of said Department before any radical change is made in its administration."

The resolutions were seconded and remarks made upon them by several members of the Chamber.

### MR. JACOB H. SCHIFF.

"While I am in favor, as Mr. Schwab knows, of the object of his resolutions, of the end he seeks to attain, I do hope that it will not be passed by this Chamber. We are entering upon dangerous ground if we take up the subject of municipal politics—if that expression is not a paradox. So long as we busy ourselves with the question of taxation, we are in our proper element; but I think it is mighty dangerous when, as a Chamber of Commerce, we take up such questions. These are questions belonging to Good Government Clubs and City Clubs, and to other semi-political societies. The Chamber of Commerce should have nothing to do with them."

John Sloane, Henry W. Cannon, and Gustav H. Schwab, to which, subsequently, Charles Stewart Smith, President of the Chamber, was added and made Chairman.

MR. CORNELIUS N. BLISS.

"It [the Police] has been a very great and valuable Department of this city, so far as the rank and file are concerned ; but during the last twelve or eighteen months we have been overwhelmed in all of the journals in this city with charges against the members of the police, especially the higher ranks of it ; and these charges go even down to the rank and file ; and I think that before we attempt to suggest even to the Legislature that we shall have a bi-partisan Police Board, or four Police Commissioners, two of each party, or before we trust the entire affairs of the Police Department to one man, whose appointment we know nothing of, we should pause and ask the Legislature to find out if the charges that have been made are true. I believe that nine-tenths of the people of this city believe that they are true, to a large extent, and I think it should be known and ascertained before we recommend any definite change."

ALEXANDER E. ORR.

"As a member of this Chamber I think I would be as jealous as any other member here to bar the door against the possibility of the introduction of any political questions into the Chamber. I think that it would be very dangerous ground ; but I think if, as merchants and citizens of New York and Brooklyn, having an interest in that which is for the benefit of the mercantile interests, and the furtherance and maintenance of the position that we have now, we keep silent when these great questions are being determined, we should be recreant to the trust that has been reposed in us, and to the position which we have always claimed to be in, that is, to be leaders in matters pertaining to commerce and to commercial interests, and that we virtually would be taking a back seat.

"Now I am one of those who hold that absolutely, from A to Z, politics has nothing to do with municipal affairs, nothing whatever. I cannot understand how a well-administered Police Board or a well-administered Fire Department has anything to do with the Democratic or Republican conditions as they obtain in national affairs. I cannot understand how under any circumstances we as merchants allow them to interfere with the management of our own business. And when we have to appoint persons who are to control those elements which define and protect our businesses and our properties and our lives, I say that when a reorganization is to be had, it is imperative upon us as thinking men, thinking merchants, fulfilling the obligations laid upon us, to come together and assert our rights and make our influence felt when we are creating the system of government which is to create this municipal management."

By the invitation of the Chamber, an address was delivered by Joel B. Erhardt, a former Commissioner of Police, discussing the bill at that time pending in the Legislature, providing for the appointment of a non-partisan Board of Police Commissioners for the city of New York, from which, however, it would not be in place to make extract here as he concerned himself rather with the organization of the Police Department than with the investigation of the police force.

### J. EDWARD SIMMONS.

" It seems to me, after the very careful presentation of this case by Colonel Erhardt, that it must be apparent to all who are here to-day that the Police Department certainly needs looking after in some way. I am in favor of this Chamber taking exactly the position that is proposed in the resolution that has been submitted, and I concur heartily with the remarks that have been made by the able Vice-President of this institution (Mr. Orr). It seems to me that the Chamber puts itself in a position where it suggests. It does not dictate, it does not say anything except what it says in the resolution that has been offered, but it suggests that an investigation be made by the proper authorities of the State. Now, if a condition prevails such as we have reason to believe does prevail, surely it is not outside or beyond the limits of this institution or its duty, to suggest to the Legislature, as proposed in the resolution that has been offered, that a committee be appointed and a legislative inquiry be instituted into the condition of affairs which we suppose exists in this city. Therefore, it seems to me entirely dignified and proper that this Chamber, which is made up of taxpayers, of men who have large interests at stake here —it seems proper that if the Police Department needs investigation it is right that this association should say so, and therefore I heartily endorse the resolution."

### A. FOSTER HIGGINS.

"I am not at all afraid that we as merchants are going out of our proper sphere of duty in arraigning these things, and in calling a spade by its name,—a spade. When we hear such stories as we do to-day about the condition of our Police Department, I feel that our liberties and our rights and our property are jeopardized, and that the merchants of this city should not be afraid to come here and say what they think about it. I cannot see any reason why we should not as a Chamber express ourselves upon a matter of such grave importance as this is to us. Politics once drove us into a civil war. We did not hesitate to come here and express our opinion on the subject, and array ourselves on the side of law and order. Now it is a question whether outlawry and disorder shall prevail in this city, or whether the city shall be properly governed."

### OSCAR S. STRAUSS.

"I hope that the question of the police investigation, so far as this Chamber is concerned, will be voted down; not because I am not in favor of it, not because I do not believe that every member here is in favor of correcting the abuses, but because it will bring into operation partisan machinery which we as a body of merchants who are of all shades of party should not be used as a rider for. While I am decidedly in favor of the division of the elections, I think that the other question we had better leave alone, for it may result that the manner in which the investigation will be carried on will produce another meeting of this Chamber, so that we may have to take a back step by reason of the investigation not being carried on in a proper manner. I hope the question will be voted down."

### CLARENCE W. BOWEN.

"I hope for the honor and credit of the Chamber of Commerce that the resolutions which have been read will be universally adopted ; we ought not to be partisans, but we ought to do what we think is our duty from a conscientious stand-point as citizens of this city, and I therefore hope that the resolutions will be unanimously adopted."

The discussion was concluded by the following address from President Charles Stewart Smith, Vice-President Orr in the chair :

"I have attended nearly every meeting of this Chamber for more than twenty-five years, excepting when I have been absent from the city. I think I have been a member of the Chamber for twenty-seven years, and I never knew a resolution offered in this Chamber with a design, or that had the effect of being a mere partisan movement. I do not think that this has any such design or will have any such effect. The question which concerns us as merchants, in my view, is this : How can laws be made, amended or defeated, which will favorably affect the commerce of this city? Now we have unanimously passed a resolution which states *that the commercial prosperity of a city is intimately connected with its government.* I believe that absolutely. I believe that our taxes are too high and that they may be made lower. I believe that the department of the city of New York (the police) that spends five millions a year, one-seventh of our whole expenses, needs investigation. I believe so from the impression that I had before Colonel Erhardt's paper was read, and my impression has been very much strengthened by that paper. Besides there are charges, more or less openly made, of grave irregularity in this department, not to use the more serious words — bribery and blackmail. Either this is true or false, and it concerns the good name of the city to know the truth. My friend Dr. Parkhurst believes the worst is true. Now I do not think that any merchants in New York need be frightened by the cry of 'politics.' I believe in a man being a practical politician ; a man of convictions can't help it — his duty demands it. I claim to be a practical politician, and always hope to be ; I am one of those who believe that the ambition of politicians should be satisfied by state and national politics and not by municipal affairs. (Applause.) Now if we want good government in this city we must have good laws which affect municipal affairs, and we are not to be scared off from the amendment of a bad law by the idea that politicians want it or don't want it. We don't want it because we are politicians, but we want it because we are citizens. I think it is time that the citizens of New York had the courage of their convictions and rose above partisanship into the higher plane of citizenship. Until then we shall have no genuine reform in municipal affairs. (Applause.)"

## CHAPTER XX

### THE SENATORIAL INVESTIGATING COMMITTEE

THE resolution of the Chamber of Commerce asking for a senatorial investigation of the Police Department was adopted January 25, 1894. In response to this action of the Chamber, and in deference to the earnest sentiment prevailing in this city, the resolution authorizing such investigation was introduced into the Senate by Senator Clarence Lexow, January 29th, and was in these terms :

" *Whereas*, It has been charged and maintained that the Police Department of the city of New York is corrupt ; that grave abuses exist in said department ; that in said city the laws for the suppression of crime and the municipal ordinances and regulations duly enacted for the peace, security, and police of said city are not strictly enforced by said Department, and by the police force acting thereunder ; that said laws and ordinances when enforced are enforced by said Department and said police force with partiality and favoritism, and that such partiality and favoritism are the result of corrupt bargains between offenders against said laws or ordinances on the one hand, and the police force on the other ; that money and promises of service to be rendered are given and paid to public officials by the keepers or proprietors of gaming-houses, disorderly houses, liquor saloons, and others who have offended or are offending against said law or ordinances in exchange for promises of immunity from punishment or police interference ; and that said Department and said police force, by means of threat and otherwise, extort money or other valuable consideration from many persons in said city as the price of such immunity from police interference or punishment for real or supposed violations of said laws and ordinances ; and

*Whereas.* A strong public sentiment demands of this Senate an investigation of all the matters above mentioned for the purpose of remedying and preventing such abuses by proper legislation ; now, therefore, be it

*Resolved,* That the President *pro tempore* of the Senate be, and he is hereby authorized to appoint seven Senators who shall be a Special Committee of this Senate, and one of whom shall be the President *pro tempore* of the Senate, with power and authority to investigate all and singular the aforesaid matters and charges, and that said Committee have full power to prosecute its inquiries in any and every direction in its judgment necessary and proper to enable it to obtain and report the information required by this resolution ; that said Committee report to the Senate with such recommendations as in its judgment the public interests require. Said Committee is given authority to send for persons and papers, to employ a stenographer and such counsel and other assistants as it may deem necessary, and to hold sessions in the cities of New York and Albany. The Committee shall conclude its investigation in time to report to the Senate on or before February 20, 1894, to the end that proper legislation may be enacted to suppress said evils. The Sergeant-at-Arms of the Senate shall attend such Committee and serve all subpœnas issued thereby, and perform all duties as Sergeant-at-Arms of such Committee. And be it further

"*Resolved*, That it is the sense of this Senate that it is contrary to public policy and to the interests of good order that any person giving evidence before said Committee leading to show that he has been a party to the practices above mentioned, should be indicted or prosecuted upon evidence so given or admissions so made by him."

On February 15, 1894, the Senate extended the time, within which the Investigating Committee was directed to make a report, to the end of the session. The time and scope of said Committee was still farther extended by subsequent action of the Senate as follows:

"*Whereas*, It appears that it is impracticable to make a report within the time so limited; therefore be it

"*Resolved*, That the said Committee, be, and it is, hereby authorized and empowered to continue the investigation in said Senate Document, No. 27, and said resolution of February 15, 1894, provided for until the next session of the Senate, in January, 1895, and that said Committee have all the power and authority during said recess conferred upon it in and by said resolution.

"*Resolved*, That said Committee be, and it hereby is, authorized and empowered, in its discretion, until the next session of the Senate in 1895, to examine and investigate the Departments of the Commissioners of Charities and Correction, Excise, and the Police Courts of the city of New York, or such of them as it may deem proper and expedient, with the same power and authority, until said next session of the Senate, conferred upon it by virtue of said resolution, and further

"*Resolved*, That such Committee be instructed to report at the next session of the Senate, and not later than January 15, 1895."

The Committee authorized by this resolution was constituted as follows :

Senators Lexow, O'Connor, Robertson, Pound, Saxton, Cantor, and Bradley.

The following telegram was received here almost immediately after the names of the Investigating Committee were announced, indicating their readiness to undertake their work, or at least their curiosity to come down and inspect our work :

"Senate Committee to Investigate Police Department of New York will meet at the Hotel Metropole Friday evening at four o'clock. Like to have you present, and ready to suggest names of counsel to conduct the investigation, from which the Committee may make its selection. We will be ready to hear testimony Saturday at ten A.M.

"CLARENCE LEXOW, *Chairman*."

The above notification was sent to the Chamber of Commerce, to the Board of Trade, and to the Society for the Prevention of Crime.

The Committee made their first appearance in town on the evening of February 1st, and convened in the parlor of the Hotel Metropole, a number of gentlemen interested in the investigation—among others, Messrs. Charles Stewart Smith, Darwin R. James, Gustav Schwab, and myself—being admitted to the conference. Probably none of us ever attended a gathering so critical in its character that was so absolutely uninteresting and hopeless. After the Committee had disposed themselves and been called to order by Mr. Lexow, the Chairman stated that they were a Senatorial Committee of Investigation, and that they were now present in their judicial capacity, and called upon Mr. Smith, as representative of the Chamber which had requested the investigation, to state his case. Mr. Smith courteously replied that he had no case, but supposed the Committee had come down to make one. The Senators gave quiet token of a sense of rebuff and of having their feelings crumpled.

"Then certainly Dr. Parkhurst has a case?" said Chairman Lexow.

With possibly less urbanity than had been exhibited by Mr. Smith, I replied that I not only had no case, but that I had serious misgivings as to the wisdom of their coming down to New York anyway.

When we remember the cordial relations which were

subsequently established, it is almost ludicrous to recall the dubious and tentative way in which we felt of each other that preliminary evening.

Up to that time the Senators had had not the slightest inkling or suspicion of what they had come down for. They had heard a good deal about the fault that some of us had been finding with the police force, and they imagined that all they had to do was to put in two days a week for the next three weeks (or till the 20th of February) sizing up the researches of the Society for the Prevention of Crime. In other words, they had come down, not to investigate the Police Department, but to investigate our investigation of it. At a late hour the Committee adjourned, in a distinctly interrogative frame of mind.

The session held the day following was of the same general complexion, only rather more so. Clear intimations of distrust were expressed by some of us, and the Committee was politely reminded that there had been a previous committee sent down from Albany on a similar errand, and that when the inquisition began to grow interesting, the committee was "called off." We ventured to suggest whether there was any danger of history repeating itself. We none of us wanted to show any disrespect to our visiting statesmen, but we had scruples against so far committing ourselves to the senatorial wave as to run the risk of being swamped if the tide should happen to go out to sea. We knew we had been working two years in accomplishing what little we had, and that it would take these seven Senators, many of them from remote parts of the State, and as ignorant of the details of the situation as though they had been born on the Pacific Slope, more than eighteen days (they were, by the terms of their resolution, to make their report to the Senate on or before the 20th of February) to get to the real inwardness of our Police Department. (It might be remarked parenthetically that they sat for nearly a year, and even then *stopped before they were through.*)

We must not make too long a story of this. We were troubled not only by the limitations of time imposed by the senatorial resolution, but even after the Committee came to a realizing sense of the fact that anything like a thorough investigation meant prolonged work on their own parts, and an extension of time beyond the date fixed by the Senate, we had to confront the troublesome question of counsel. The name of almost every prominent lawyer in the city was canvassed. No one seemed anxious to touch the case. Some of those who were approached questioned the sincerity of the Committee. Some doubted if a case could be made against the police. Some were afraid of incurring the displeasure of Tammany Hall. In some instances there was hesitancy to believe that counsel's fees would ever be paid, it being remembered that one legal gentleman who had served in a similar capacity had never had his bill honored by the State, and there was some reasonable question whether Governor Flower would ever endorse an appropriation bill that looked to the exploiting of Tammany Hall. In almost all the above instances Mr. Goff's name had been mentioned as associate counsel, but his phenomenal fitness for the position was not at that time sufficiently suspected to allow of his being largely considered for the position of first counsel. The chivalrous stand which he had taken in the Gardner trial, as already referred to, as well as the signal ability he at that time displayed, easily secured the confidence of those of us who had known him in that connection, and it came about after a little, that the judgment of those, whose opinions weighed in the matter, more and more gathered about him, and he became the general choice, subject only to the condition that relations mutually satisfactory could be agreed upon between him and the members of the Lexow Committee. This last, however, was a result not easily compassed. Mr. Goff was a Democrat, and five members of the Committee were Republicans; Mr. Goff was obstinate, and so were the Committee, and neither trusted the other.

Aside from all that, there were secret political influences at work, of which I have documentary proof in my possession, aiming to subordinate the investigation to political ends. All of that matter we shall best pass over, however. Mr. Smith and myself made a special trip to Albany to the end of mediating between Mr. Goff and the Committee. He suspected them, and they considered him dictatorial. We carried up with us the following statement of conditions which Mr. Goff, Mr. Smith, and myself had agreed that he ought to insist upon :

" First, that the authority of the Senate to the Committee to continue the investigation after the adjournment of the Legislature shall be made absolute.

"Second, that thirty days intervene before the Committee give public hearing, and that the sittings thereafter be as nearly as possible from day to day.

" Third, that Mr. Goff have privilege of selecting the associate counsel, with the approval of the Committee.

" Fourth, that counsel may employ such clerical and other assistance as may be deemed necessary in the prosecution of the inquiry.

" Fifth, that the Committee shall furnish ways and means to maintain a proper and efficient service during the whole of the inquiry.

" Sixth, that counsel be not restricted or limited in the scope of the investigation, but shall be free to push all lines of inquiry which may be relevant or pertinent to the letter and spirit of the resolution of the committee."

We told Mr. Lexow, in Albany, that if the terms of agreement, as drawn up by us gentlemen, seemed to him stringent, he must remember that they were drafted by men who were breathing an atmosphere of utter distrust in him and in all of his Committee. We told them that they could trust Mr. Goff, and then we came back to New York and told Mr. Goff that he could trust them.

The question was finally settled on a critical Saturday morning in Mr. Goff's office. Mr. Smith, Mr. Goff, and myself will doubtless always remember the scene. Mr. Goff recently described it graphically at a public dinner. Mr. Smith drove and I coaxed, and between us both the noble Irishman succumbed, and the destiny of the Senatorial Investigating Committee was settled.

The Sutherland episode it is perhaps just as well not to rehearse. W. A. Sutherland, Esq., an honorable gentleman and an excellent lawyer, but as ignorant of the situation here in New York as though he had been reared in South America, was, for inscrutable purposes, brought upon the scene from Western New York, to be counsel to the Committee, without any precise definition of the relations which were to subsist between him and Mr. Goff. It threatened at one time to wreck the investigation, but little by little his personal presence faded out from among us, and his connection with the investigation has shrunk into an impalpable memory. We attribute to him none but the highest motives, but his introduction into the case was, on the part of the Committee, or, perhaps, it should be said, on the part of certain parties outside who exercised a dominating influence over certain members of the Committee, a mistake, and for a time sadly rasped the nervous irritability of a community that was on the constant verge of scepticism touching the investigation and all that pertained to it.

The Senate Committee commenced to take evidence on March 9th, limiting themselves, however, for the time, to the matter of election frauds. The inquisition proper, however, did not begin till Mr. Goff's appearance, more than two months later.

Mr. Delancey Nicoll had been retained by certain of the police officials to protect their imperilled interests before the Committee. But as Chairman Lexow introduced the investigation by an assertion of the position, that the Committee would not be bound by the ordinary rules of evidence, and would let in everything that would help to illuminate the situation, it did very little good for Nicoll to "Object;" and either because he found himself hampered by the conditions under which he would have to act, or for other reasons not understood by the public, he soon withdrew. We were all sorry to bid him good-by, for his pleasantries relieved the tension of the inquisition and infused into the tragic character of the sessions those veins of light comedy that helped to variegate and to brighten the earnestness of the situation. We got along a good deal faster after he had gone, but still we missed him.

The Committee adjourned on April 14th, not to convene again until after the adjournment of the Legislature.

The Committee reconvened, and earnest solid work

was commenced on the 21st of May, Mr. Goff being counsel-in-chief, and Messrs. Frank Moss and William Travers Jerome being associate counsel.

The Senate Bill appropriating $25,000 to meet the expense of the investigation, had, in the meantime, been vetoed by Governor Flower in terms that dishonored his position even if not himself, and that showed his moral inability to sink a partisan in the statesman. The stupendous revelations that have issued from the investigation are a sad commentary on his gubernatorial blunder, and on the ignominious phrases in which he saw fit to put his blunder before the public.

It is foreign to the purpose of our narrative to follow the details of the investigation as it proceeded from this point, with occasional suspensions, until the eve of our recent election. Some reference will be made to it in our concluding chapter. There is nothing that parallels it, so far as we are aware, in the moral history of our race. Although the Senate Committee entered upon its work with no suspicion of what their work would involve, it faithfully and steadily stood behind Mr. Goff as he mercilessly pressed the inquisitorial probe into the quivering vitals of the body politic ; and as for Mr. Goff, although he committed himself to the service of the Committee with exceeding misgiving and only in response to importunate entreaty, once his affirmative decision was reached, he threw himself into the work

with self-regardless and self-consuming devotion, and so
did honor to his profession, created for himself a national
name, and unsuspectingly discovered to his fellow-
citizens the man whom they could agree with enthusiastic accord to elevate to the Recorder's bench. It was
the Lexow Committee, Mr. Goff, and his associates—
who, though less conspicuous, were as faithful as he—
that put the cap-sheaf to the work of the two previous
years, showed the inwardness of the situation and
touched the popular heart so deeply that minor considerations passed out of view, and the intelligent conscience of an aroused municipality could bind itself
together to the nomination and election of a Mayor
whose only purpose it is to serve God and his city.

## CHAPTER XXI

### THE COMMITTEE OF SEVENTY *

THE summer of 1894 found the citizens of New York in an unwonted state of agitation and excitement on the subject of the condition of their municipal government, and the character of the individuals controlling the operations of its several departments.

The supineness and lack of public spirit exhibited, during a series of years, by those having most at stake, had permitted every department of the city government to be filled by the appointees of Tammany Hall.

This organization, while nominally Democratic, was composed of, and controlled by, men drawn together by the sole object of fattening upon the control of city offices.

The patronage of such offices was used to reward the members of the organization and others who could be induced to co-operate with and support them.

New York City has always been largely Democratic in national politics, and Tammany Hall, calling itself Democratic, by means of the thoroughness of its or-

* This chapter has been prepared for us by the great courtesy of Joseph Larocque, Esq., President of the Committee of Seventy.

ganization, had succeeded in having itself recognized as the regular Democratic organization of the city, in Conventions of the Democratic party. Democrats who believed in the principles of their party, and considered the success of those principles of paramount importance when election-day arrived, while condemning the course pursued in city affairs, felt constrained to vote their party ticket, fearing that, by pursuing any other course, injury might result to the national cause.

In this way Tammany Hall had been permitted to perpetuate, extend, and consolidate its power.

Long toleration and success had made its leaders bold, and during the six preceding years the character of these appointments to office had steadily deteriorated.

Notes of warning had been sounded from time to time. Mr. Godkin, in the *Evening Post*, had called attention to the existing conditions and tendencies, and to the danger of permitting Grant to be elected Mayor, and had day by day endeavored to arouse our citizens to a sense of their impending danger ; but the citizens were too much occupied with their own private affairs to pay much attention to the government of their city.

About the beginning of 1892, Dr. Parkhurst having satisfied himself that a system prevailed, under which, in consideration of tribute paid to officials, vice and crime were protected by the Police Department, had entered upon his crusade. In spite of hostile criticisms and obstacles of every description interposed in his way, Dr. Parkhurst had succeeded in uncovering the corruption of the Police Department sufficiently to secure the appointment of a Legislative Committee of Investigation.

The Lexow Committee had proceeded day by day, in the work of investigation, each day bringing to light some new evidence of corruption, until the close of the summer of 1894 found the citizens at last thoroughly aroused to the necessity of action.

That conditions of corruption and maladministration analogous to those developed in the Police Department would be found to exist in other Departments few doubted.

The question of the hour was, How could this condition be changed? How could the so-called political organization which had secured absolute control of the whole machinery of the city government be overthrown?

The Democratic party in the city was split up into several distinct organizations, all hostile to Tammany Hall, and each jealous of the others, and especially jealous and distrustful of the Republicans.

The Republican party itself was not a unit, and, judging from the past, was not to be relied upon to unite with the Democrats opposed to Tammany Hall in support of a ticket put in nomination by them.

Tammany Hall ordinarily controlled more votes

than either the Republicans or the Independent Democrats.

With three tickets in the field Tammany Hall would be almost certain to succeed through the thoroughness of its organization, its control of patronage, and its power to oppress its opponents.

Experience has shown that in view of the distrust and jealousy entertained by each of the existing political organizations toward the others, there was little hope of any overture by one to the others for joint action being successful.

In this situation a number of citizens, realizing the vital importance of a concerted effort at the coming election on the part of all who desired to overthrow the existing corrupt control of public affairs, and to place the government of the city in the hands of reputable, capable men, who could be relied upon to administer it on sound, honest, business principles, in the last days of August issued a call for a meeting of citizens, irrespective of party, to be held at the Madison Square Garden Concert Hall, on Thursday, September 6, 1894.

This call was as follows:

"NEW YORK, August 28, 1894.

"DEAR SIR: You are invited to attend a meeting of the citizens of New York, irrespective of party, to be held at the Madison Square Garden Concert or Recital Hall, on Thursday, September 6th, at eight o'clock.

"This meeting is called to consult as to the wisdom and practicability of taking advantage of the present state of public feeling, to organize a citizens' movement for the government of the city of New York, entirely outside of party politics, and solely in the interest of efficiency, economy, and the public health, comfort, and safety.

"It is believed that the people of the city are tired of the burden of inefficiency, extravagance, and plunder, and understand that a city, like a well-ordered household, should be managed solely in the best interests of its people, and to this end should be entirely divorced from party politics and selfish personal ambition or gain.

W. Bayard Cutting,
Charles S. Smith,
George F. Baker,
Charles Butler,
James Speyer,
G. G. Williams,
W. L. Strong,
C. Vanderbilt,
William H. Webb,
J. Harsen Rhoades,
Alfred S. Heidelbach,
Morris K. Jessup,
William Mertens,
W. E. Dodge,
H. C. Fahnestock,
Hugh N. Camp,

H. Cillis,
George Macculloch Miller,
Julius J. Frank,
Woodbury Langdon,
Henry Rice,
F. D. Tappen,
J. Crosby Brown,
Max J. Lissauer,
John P. Townsend,
William Ottmann,
Joseph Larocque,
George W. Quintard,
M. S. Fecheimer,
G. Norrie,
James M. Constable,
Gustav H. Schwab,
A. S. Frissell."

On the date named, in response to this call, there was a gathering of some hundreds of citizens.

The meeting was organized by the selection of a Chairman and Secretary.

Letters were read from many prominent citizens who were unable to be present, expressing sympathy with the objects of the meeting. There was an interchange of views, and speeches were made by several of those present. An address was unanimously adopted, which was as follows, viz.:

"*To the People of the City of New York, Regardless of Party:*

"Convincing proofs of corruption in important municipal departments of this city have been presented; inefficiency, ignorance, and extravagance in public affairs are apparent, and business principles in the conduct of the affairs of this municipality are set aside and neglected for private gain and partisan advantage. The present government of this city is a standing menace to the continued commercial supremacy of the metropolis, and strongly concerns the welfare of every family in the whole country, for there is no hamlet in the land that the influence of New York City does not reach for good or evil.

The time has come for a determined effort to bring about such a radical and lasting change in the administration of the city of New York as will insure the permanent removal of the abuses from which we suffer, and the management of the affairs of the city as a well-ordered household, solely in the interests of its people. Municipal government should be entirely divorced from party politics, and selfish, personal ambition or gain. The economical, honest, and businesslike management of municipal affairs has nothing to do with questions of national or State politics. We do not ask any citizen to give up his party on national or State issues, but to rise above partisanship to the broad plane of citizenship, and to unite in an earnest demand for the nomination and election of fitting candidates, whatever their national party affiliations, and to form a citizens' movement for the government of this city entirely outside of party politics, and only in the interest of efficiency, economy, and public health, comfort, and safety.

"We pledge our active co-operation with all other organizations of this city holding the same purposes and aims, recognizing that only through a combined and well-organized effort of all citizens who desire good government can that object be attained."

The meeting also adopted the following resolution, viz.:

"*Resolved*, That a Committee of Seventy, of which the Chairman and the Secretary shall be members, be appointed by the Chair, with full power to confer with other Anti-Tammany organizations, and to take such action as may be necessary to further the objects of this meeting, as set forth in the call therefor, and the address adopted by this meeting."

Under the authority conferred by this resolution the Chair appointed the "Committee of Seventy."

Its membership represents every shade of opinion in national politics and all classes of citizens.

The first meeting of the "Committee of Seventy" was held at the rooms of the Chamber of Commerce of the State of New York, on September 19, 1894.

An organization was then perfected, and an Executive Committee and a Finance Committee appointed.

Full powers were conferred upon the Executive Committee to carry out the objects of the organization.

The Executive Committee, like the General Committee, was composed of men of all shades of opinion on national questions; all agreeing, however, on one point, viz., That no question of national politics was involved or should enter into the administration of city affairs.

They proceeded to frame a platform on which they could all unite, and which any candidates whom they might put in nomination must accept.

This platform was as follows, viz.:

### THE COMMITTEE OF SEVENTY'S PLATFORM.

"We reiterate the following principles, contained in the Address to the People of the City of New York, heretofore issued.

"*Municipal government should be entirely divorced from party politics and from selfish personal ambition or gain.*

"*The economical, honest, and business-like management of municipal affairs has nothing to do with questions of national or State politics.*

"We do not ask any citizen to give up his party on national or State issues, but to rise above partisanship to the broad plane of citizenship, and to unite in an earnest demand for the nomination and election of fitting candidates, whatever their national party affiliations.

" The government of the city of New York, in the hands of its present administrators, is marked by corruption, inefficiency, and extravagance ; its municipal departments are not conducted in the interests of the city at large, but for private gain and partisan advantage.

" All classes of citizens, rich and poor alike, suffer under these conditions. This misgovernment endangers the health and morality of the community, and deprives its citizens of the protection of life and property to which they are entitled.

" The call goes to the citizens of New York to face the dangers that confront them, and resolutely to determine that these conditions shall cease, and that the affairs of the city shall henceforth be conducted as a well-ordered, efficient, and economical household, in the interests of the health, comfort, and safety of the people.

" **We denounce as repugnant to the spirit and letter of our institutions any discriminations among citizens because of race or religious belief.**

" We demand that the public service of this city be conducted upon a strictly non-partisan basis ; that all subordinate appointments and promotions be based on Civil Service Examinations, and that all examinations, mental and physical, be placed under the control of the Civil Service Commission.

"*We demand that the quality of the Public Schools be improved, their capacity enlarged, and proper playgrounds provided, so that every child within the ages required by law shall have admission to the Schools, the health of the children be protected, and that all such modern improvements be introduced as will make our Public Schools the equal of those in any other city in the world.*

"*We insist that the property already acquired by the city under the Small Park Act shall be promptly devoted to the purposes of this acquisition, so that our people in the densely populated parts of our city shall fully enjoy the benefits of such expenditures.*

"*We urge greater care and thoroughness in the enforcement of the health laws, and demand the establishment of more efficient safeguards against disease.*

"*We favor the establishment of adequate public baths and lavatories for the promotion of cleanliness and increased public comfort, at appropriate places throughout the city.*

"*We demand the adoption of a thorough system of street cleaning, which shall also include a proper disposition of the refuse and garbage, so that our harbor may be kept free from obstruction and defilement and the neighboring shores clear of offal, thus conforming to the methods in other great cities.*

"*We call for increased rapid transit facilities in this city.*

"We call for the improvement of the docks and water-fronts of our great maritime city, so that it shall enjoy the advantages to which it is entitled by its unique position with its unrivalled harbor.

"We heartily favor the separation of municipal from State and national elections, and a larger measure of home rule for cities.

"**We appeal to the people of this city to cast aside party prejudice and to combine with us in a determined effort to elect candidates chosen solely with reference to their ability and integrity, and pledged to conduct the affairs of this city on a strictly non-partisan basis, and who will, as far as may be in their power, insure good government to the city of New York.**"

The Executive Committee appointed a Conference Committee to meet with the representatives of all other Anti-Tammany organizations. Many conferences were held and views exchanged as to the general policy to be pursued most likely to secure union and success.

Finally the Executive Committee put in nomination candidates for the following offices, viz.: Mayor, President of Board of Aldermen, Judge of the Superior Court of the City of New York, Sheriff, and two Coroners.

Pursuant to a resolution previously adopted the gentleman selected as the candidate for Mayor being in national politics a Republican, the residue of the ticket, with the exception of one of the Coroners, was made up of gentlemen who in national politics were Democrats.

The nominations so made were approved by the

General Committee, and finally accepted by all the other Anti-Tammany organizations—Democratic and Republican.

Each of the candidates named expressly approved of the principles of the platform adopted, and agreed to be governed by those principles in the administration of his office, if elected, and further, that in making appointments he would be guided by considerations of character and capacity alone, and not by party lines.

From the time when these nominations were made to the day of election, the Campaign Committee, composed of the Executive Committee and the Finance Committee, gave themselves up to the work of the campaign, holding almost daily meetings. Headquarters were established in a house hired for the purpose, in charge of one of their members selected as manager, and of their Sub-Committee on publication.

Frequent conferences were held with representatives of the various organizations which had accepted their candidates, and public meetings were had under the auspices of the Committee.

Information as to the situation was furnished to the press from day to day, and reviews of the misleading statements of facts and figures, put forth by the Tammany managers, were carefully prepared and given to the public.

A force of watchers at the polls was organized under the direction of the Committee, composed largely of members of the Good Government Clubs, so that each of the 1,141 Election Districts was provided on election day with competent and reliable watchers, interested to see that the election was fairly conducted.

Proclamations offering rewards for information leading to the conviction of offenders against the election laws were posted and distributed.

Paster ballots, containing the names of the candidates of the Committee, in combination with the candidates of the several political parties for State offices and members of Assembly, were distributed to all the registered voters in the city by mail, and were furnished to the various organizations supporting the candidates of the Committee, for use on election day.

No pains were spared to bring to the attention of every voter the momentous character of the issues involved, and to stimulate his action in support of a pure, honest, non-partisan administration of our municipal government.

These efforts, with the loyal, hearty support of the several organizations in sympathy with the movement inaugurated by the Committee of Seventy, were crowned with success on election day.

The result is full of promise to the friends of good government.

By the recent amendments to the Constitution of our State under which municipal elections hereafter are to be held in different years from State and federal elections, the road is made more easy for the election in the future of candidates of character and fitness for the positions for which they may be put in nomination, and for maintaining the administration of our municipal affairs on a clean, business-like, non-partisan basis.

To accomplish these results, however, untiring vigilance, on the part of all interested in the cause of good government, is indispensable.

## CHAPTER XXII

### ELECTION APPEAL FROM THE MADISON SQUARE PULPIT

The roots of this entire movement, as it has been thus far portrayed, have been in the churches and synagogues. The first note struck was to the conscience, and that note has been sounded persistently through to the end. It has seemed, therefore, proper to introduce at this point, the discourse preached from my pulpit on November 4th—two days before our recent election ; not at all because of any novelty in the facts which it presents, but because it aims to string those facts upon a thread of eternal principle, and to posit the possibility of thorough reconstruction, socially and municipally, upon the grounds occupied by the Prophets and Apostles.

#### THE DISCOURSE.

"*Turn ye again now every one from his evil way, and from the evil of your doings, and dwell in the land that the Lord hath given unto you and to your fathers for ever and ever.*"—JEREMIAH XXV. 5.

The circumstances under which we meet this morning afford all in the way of preface that the occasion requires. Those who understand the situation best, are the ones who will most clearly appreciate the seriousness of the crisis through which, not only municipally, but also nationally, we are just now passing; and we may say not only nationally, but even universally, for tangible evidence of the anxious interest taken in this struggle has reached us, not only from England and the Continent of Europe, but from Asia, and from as far away as Tasmania, away around on the opposite side of the globe.

As the conflict has progressed and the issue has been made clear, it has become evident that the forces which are now contending with each other here are forces broader in their scope and longer in their intent than such as concern themselves with any single town or year; rather that they are the energies of good and evil—as long as the years and as wide as the world—which everywhere confront each other, but which just now are marshalled in concentrated warfare upon the arena of our own municipality.

These things have been stated here before, you will remember, but their prior statement was open to the charge of being mixed with elements of theory and supposition. But the supposititious stage is past. We stand down now on the clear, open ground of absolute demonstration. The facts in the case are known. They are known and they are appreciated, and the grounds of conviction lie out easily in sight and are matter of record. So that to-day when we say that the *personnel* of our city government is a quotation from every species of criminal that rotten civilization is able to produce, or the devil able to invent, we are simply asserting a commonplace that the moral intelligence of the entire country is prepared enthusiastically to consent to, and that can be stated to-day with no more fear of its provoking a presentment or an indictment, than though I were to repeat the Sermon on the Mount, or the Ten Laws that Moses brought down from the top of Sinai. It has taken a good while to do it, but it is done and will stay done. History can never go back of it, and we are by so much nearer the millennium in consequence of it. How long it will take to cover the balance of the distance is not the question. The river ends in the sea, and the river is making ground. Praise ye the Lord!

And it is this moral property that makes out the distinctness of the present issue. The outlines of the conflict are as sharply marked as they were in the duel waged between Christ and Satan in the wilderness, and for the same reason. There is nothing in this campaign that does not come home as directly and easily to an ignorant man as it does to an instructed one ; to a foreigner, as it does to a native ; to a poor man, as it does to a wealthy one. It is not a matter of capital ; it is not a question of policy ; it is not an affair of thinking, reasoning, or philosophising. It is a question of what is right and what is wrong. Conscience is the one only particular faculty that comes just now into play ; and the moral element is the strength of the whole movement and has been all the way through. That is why we none of us were obliged to make a specific study of political economy before entering into the conflict, except to the extent that the Commandments make out the biggest half of any system of political economy that has vigor enough to hold its own and win its way. That is why the self-respecting element of community has all come into solid coalition in this movement with the understanding that all side considerations shall be postponed. When righteousness has been established in this city the air will still bristle with difficult questions without doubt, and questions that conscience alone will not suffice to answer save as it is aided by experience, by research, and by careful balancing of counter-considerations ; but there is nothing of that here. There is nothing in the movement immediately in hand that calls for anything just now, or that will call for anything this week, but a conscience to feel the right, and a moral purpose to carry the discernment of conscience into effect. In other words, avoid it as you like, and wince under it as you please, the election in this city next Tuesday will practically be nothing more nor less than a public vote on the Ten Commandments.

The history of this city, therefore, has reached a point of moral crisis. The general facts in the case are not so much better known than they were two years ago, but those facts have been so pared down to sharp edges and acute angles that there is no longer any way to avoid seeing them, and have been so pushed into the tissue of the general consciousness that that consciousness is stirred to reflection and compelled to action. There is nothing truer than the statement that has been reiteratedly made by parties that are themselves involved in these iniquities, that matters are in no worse shape now than they have been for a good many years. More than two years ago people well versed in the municipal situation were saying, "These things are all true, but what are you going to do about it?" The staggering point in the situation was its moral lifelessness—pricking the conscience produced no pain. We were suffering from ethical bankruptcy. We were being ruled by beasts, and yet it did not hurt our feelings. Our moral cuticle had become seared down to the situation.

I am not speaking now of the conscience of our rulers—take them as they run, they haven't any; at least any that is available for ethical effects. We have it from them directly that they cannot understand what this that we call "moral indignation" is all about. All that crime means to them is the liability of being sent to Sing Sing for it. With them remorse is a lost art. I am not saying that there are not exceptions to this. I am simply saying that, taken as a whole, the herd that is preying on us is composed of a lot of moral incapables that have breathed iniquity, eaten iniquity, drunk iniquity, and bartered in iniquity so long that to them iniquity is actually the normal condition of things, as propriety and decency are normal to the estimate of people that live righteously.

But that is not the worst part of the matter by any manner of means. The worst part of the matter is that it has struck a kind of moral paralysis into the heart of community at large. Now this is the moral mire out of which we are slowly emerging. One of the most thrilling experiences which I have had in this entire campaign was the enthusiastic applause which greeted a public utterance that I recently made to the Ten Commandments. The idea of a big New York audience, in the heat of a political campaign, giving three cheers for the Decalogue, is—I don't know what it is—there is no word that will quite cover the situation.

Now conceive to yourselves the strategic character of the moment, and the unspeakable opportunity that will this week be at the command of the God-fearing people of this town, of taking this intensified condition of moral sentiment and sticking a pin in it and making it a permanent fixture of our municipal character and the character of our municipal government. Here is a chance to lift the chariot wheels out of the muddy ruts of human villainy and filth, and set them down on the hard, ringing pavement of the mind and will of God. That is what this election stands for—and it is all that it stands for. That is why we bring this matter into the church, and there is no place where it is so perfectly and appropriately at home as in the church. I declare to you that I cannot understand how there can be a preacher in this city, provided only he has crawled far enough out of his clerical shell to know what is going on, and provided he has not been so celestially sublimated as to be oblivious of the terrestrial condition that our holy religion is given for no other purpose but to take hold of and improve, can let slip the super-eminent opportunity of sounding a tone that shall transfix the situation, and pierce to the vitals of the individual and collective conscience.

New York is going to be morally exalted this week or it is going to be morally blighted. There can be done in one week of crisis what cannot be done in an entire year when there is no crisis on hand. The circumstances here in New York to-day are no different from those recorded in the Old Testament times. There is just as much reason why every preacher in this city—Protestant, Catholic, and Hebrew—should be a Jeremiah to-day as there was why Jeremiah should be a Jeremiah in his day, dealing Titanic blows upon the organized iniquity of the Baal-worshippers and treacherous scoundrels, who trod under foot precisely the same laws that are being crushed into the earth by the conscienceless and godless criminals who are determining our city's history and destiny. There is just as much politics in the way Jeremiah handled his times as there is in the way I am handling our times, and there is not a shred of politics in either.

If I cared to step aside and say anything just now about the matter of a revival of religion, I would declare that even the possibilities of a revival are limited by the responsiveness of the conscience that the reviving spirit has to deal with. Conscience lies at the basis of the entire situation. Preaching is effective only as there is a responsive conscience to preach to. The Holy Ghost can work only as there is a conscience to work upon. When I come before a congregation I feel that there is no opportunity for effect save as there is that in the hearts of the hearers upon which words of truth and admonition can hook themselves. There can be only so much moral power in the speaker as there is moral hook in the hearer. The power in the pulpit is measured by the conscience in the pew. I assure you there is nothing we preachers feel so crowding a need of right in the church as conscience; the sharp, sensitive response to that which is righteous; and now here is an opportunity this week, by a single consummate stroke, to make righteousness a big reality to the stimulated sensibilities of an aroused community, and to send forth a tone that shall collect the scattered notes of human estimate into a sublime chord that shall go ringing through the city and country, and down the years.

Let us also clearly understand, just at this point of our discussion, that it is not a question whether things have not for a considerable time past been equally as bad as they are now. That is one of the lines of defence that is being pursued by certain of the wretched official protectors of public virtue against whom our warfare is directed. The District-Attorney's office—the pivot upon which, according to repute, there hinges as much in the way of travesty of justice as in any other single department of our city government — the District - Attorney's office, through its chief exponent, has just given the public to understand that the present situation is substantially identical with what it has been for a number of previous administrations. Supposing that it be true—we may have our own opinion as to whether it *is* true— but *supposing* it to be true, that does not touch the matter. Supposing there were an open cesspool down on City Hall Square, and that it had been there for ten years, yes, for a hundred years, and that as the principles of sanitation began to take scientific shape, men should begin to look more and more quizzically at that cesspool, and to resent with increasing seriousness its mal-odorousness and its fetid and typhoid-fever-producing properties ; to what degree do you think it would satisfy the intelligent sense of community to be told that it was an indignity to the pool to find fault with it, that it smelt no worse, and caused no more mortality than it had been doing for half a century ? Now that is exactly what we have down there on City Hall Square, an open cesspool (moral cesspool), and its fatality is not diminished nor its ethical stench sweetened by its having said for it that it has been polluting the air for ten years, or even for a hundred years. There are developing in community, certain strenuous convictions as to municipal sewerage, and we are trying simply to contrive a system of piping that shall drain that political quagmire, and see if we cannot get rid of the odor, the mire, and the fever-germs ; and the length of time that it has been lying there is neither interesting nor pertinent.

I want now, that you who are parents should reflect upon what all this municipal condition means in its relation to your children. You were told here, almost three long years ago, that it is your boys that are at stake. The influences with which the air is saturated are boring into and honeycombing the tissue of young integrity. That which is wrong cannot be treated as though it were right without working in the conscience a certain amount of paralysis. There is nothing more insidiously fatal to a boy's prospective manhood than to gain an early impression that the difference between a straight line and a line that is not quite straight, is more an affair of imagination than it is of fact. Now a law that is simply set up to be played with is nothing more nor less than a conscience-pulverizer. A man who is in very close alliance with the liquor interest in this town, but who, for all that, believes in law and in its enforcement, and who appreciates distinctly the fact that there is nothing that will abstract from a young person moral virility like letting him imagine that law is not a fact but a fiction, recently told me this anecdote of his own boy:

"Father," said he, "that liquor saloon is open and it is Sunday, and the law says it shall not be open Sunday. Father, what is law anyway?"

Now the budding conception in that little chap's mind, that law really means nothing in particular, was a small shove toward his perdition. The possibilities of ruin, temporal and everlasting, are involved in any conception of law that does not load it with ingredients of the immutable and the eternal. And because in this community law is not handled as though it had its grounds in the eternal, nor truth dealt with other than as nine-pins set up to be bowled down, nor principle in general treated as possessing the power of an endless life and abiding from everlasting to everlasting, character is despoiled of its virility, and vivid conscience and muscular integrity are tending to become a matter of memory and of record only, not a present potency working among us in stern but sustaining imperialism.

But still more productive of young irresolution and degeneracy is the presence in our midst of men who are officially exalted, but yet whom we know to be personally vile—individual incarnations of every imaginable breach of commandment, whether of God or man. It does not lie within the range of possibility that we should have a mayor, or judges, or the heads of important and responsible departments who are either themselves individually tainted, or who are in transparent and eminent sympathy with those who are so tainted, without that fact operating with the power of an irresistible and incurable blight in particular upon young men who grow up with an instinctive respect for high official position, and who, therefore, cannot contemplate the occupant of such a position, however confessedly vicious and contemptible, without to a degree identifying the position and the man who fills it, and letting some of the dignity of the place insinuate itself into his conception of the functionary, and varnishing with the semblance of grace that functionary's dishonor. When you tell over the inventory of the murderers, thieves, perjurers, bribe-takers, defaulters, drunkards, and libertines that are discharging high official function in this city to-day, remember that each of them helps to make murder, theft, debauchery, and all the rest, a little less repulsive to the moral taste of your dear boy; and when you go to the polls on Tuesday, think that over.

But it is not only as parents, but as patriots also that you have to consider this matter. You cannot look intently and passionately into the situation of our own city at this juncture without feeling that in a very true and momentous sense the condition and prospects of the entire country are implicated in it. There is not a town of any considerable size in the Union that is not going to be either ennobled or degraded by our own municipal issue on Tuesday. Just that relation is appreciated, and in many instances with painful intensity. If we weaken Satan's grip on

New York this week, there are anxious spirits scattered all through the country that will be saying on Wednesday morning: "Well! if they can do it in New York, we can do it in our town." And they will do it. A successful blow struck for God and the right here on Manhattan Island will create a thousand echoes far and wide across the continent, and mean politics will look meaner, and filthy politicians will look filthier, and elevated statesmanship will appear grander to the mind and heart of every honest American. Everything is possible when once you have seen it done. There are no lessons like object-lessons. It is simple statement of historic fact to say that there are hundreds of movements, similar to the one here in progress, that have been initiated at the impulse of the movement here, and every one of these movements is going to precipitate itself in a long leap toward consummation if they see the efforts of this city culminating in success. His must be a dead soul—a hundred times dead—that is not thrilled with the gigantic impulse of such a consideration. It is as though you were able to put yourself at the heart of this great body politic and produce an influence that should strengthen the pulse-beat in each separate vein and artery of the system.

This reference to the national bearings of our present situation suggests a point which needs to be made carefully, but which I am sure can be made safely if it is made outspokenly. One special phase of current national anxiety has its grounds in the wide prevalence at home and abroad of what is scientifically known as anarchy; and when it was intimated some days ago that there was a movement among certain anarchists in this city, looking to a combination for the replacement of our present city government by one that was better, the instant conclusion in certain quarters appears to have been that it was the latest instance out of Beelzebub trying to cast out Beelzebub. Without having taken a brief for the anarchists, and with no intention at all of pleading for their eccentric method of reforming history, I submit to your consideration that there are anarchists, and there are anarchists. The genius of anarchy you understand, of course, is nothing more nor less than defiance of law. Now while clearly there cannot be very much said in behalf of a system that starts with the abandonment of all system, yet defiance of law may be overt, or it may be covert. It may parade with red flags, or it may have the parade and omit the flags. As a general principle the red-bannered procession is to be preferred, for then you know precisely who is who, and what is what. If they omit the banners they may still be anarchists, but you may take them for nuns marching to a convent, or monks trooping to a monastery, or mayors, aldermen, judges, and commissioners administering a city government. It clears the air, therefore, and simplifies matters vastly if they go well badged. Now if there is anything that the Senate Committee has succeeded in demonstrating to this city, particularly during the week past, and yesterday, it is that the corporation of political reptiles that is administering this city, has for its genius, contempt for everything that is fixed and determinate, and that the outward ceremonies of legality under which it conducts its operations are simply the thin and sneaking disguise with which it seeks to mask its anarchical defiance of everything which is statutory; in other words, that the nerve and tissue of the system is anarchy in its essence, and of as pure a type as ever was produced in Chicago or St. Petersburg, but unencumbered by bunting, tricked out in the millinery of legality, lacking in the ingenuousness of anarchy of the ordinary type, but on that account more perilous because more insidious, as man shrinks with colder horror from a slimy serpent than he does from a frank and honest gorilla. Anarchy of the ingenuous order plants hard blows upon the mailed front of civilization; anarchy of the Tammany type is every whit as defiant of law, but clandestinely introduces its subtile virus into the tissue of civilization. Oh! the red-flagged style is vastly to be preferred.

But there is that in the situation which extends our thoughts even beyond national frontiers. It is not American conceit or bravado that prompts us to feel that cis-Atlantic civilization is appointed to play an important *rôle* in the history and development of the nations at large; but we are not as a nation going to be able permanently to communicate impulses that we do not ourselves nationally incarnate. We are not going to be permanently able with our morals and our religion to work foreign results of a finer type than those which we are able by the same morals and religion to produce at home. What we are, will be the measure of what we can do, nationally exactly as much as individually. The heathen have already begun to be suspicious of religion imported from America, which shows itself under such hideous forms of development in so many visitors from America; and if America, if New York, has not in its Christianity virile tension sufficient to subdue its own heathen and protect itself from its own outlaws, it will lack just those credentials needed to secure its hospitable reception and entertainment in Pekin and Madagascar.

In every aspect, then, under which we may survey the situation, our hearts beat with high anticipation in the same instant in which we tremble with unspeakable solicitude. If a few loop-holes of insight, that have been almost accidentally gained into the unfathomed depths of pollution in which our municipality is officially reeking, have brought to view so much that is loathsome and unutterable, what must we imagine would be the full story of dishonor, if it could be told in the horror of all its details? And one thing that we have to remember is, that with the nation as with the individual, sin, when it is finished, bringeth forth death. There is no power, even in the might of God, to recover a people, and set it again upon a high track of destiny, when it has once reached a certain point of moral decay. History declares that, with a directness and with an emphasis of reiteration that is overwhelming and appalling. You can love your country and work for it, and pray and plead for it, but there is a stage of rottenness which, when once reached, the country is damned already beyond the power of the Holy Ghost to do anything for it. If you do not fancy that way of stating it, you can look into your Bibles or examine profane history generally, and find the matter put, perhaps, in a manner more to your liking; but the *matter* is the same. National sin means national poison, and the unstemmed progress of national disease means eventual national death; it always has and always will, and God will make no exception in behalf of the Western Continent. If there is no way of staying the tide of pollution that is setting with so full and oozy a current, as has been repulsively demonstrated in our own town, if, I say, there is no way of stopping it, there is not much remaining for us to do but wait for destiny and pray for the Lord to take us before the year of destiny comes. Although I had some lively suspicions as to the real condition of affairs when I first spoke to you upon the matter two years ago last February, I confess that, at that time, my worst presentiments hardly more than grazed the actuality as it has since been disclosed; and I do profoundly thank the Lord for the stimulating obstructions that were put in our way by the canting hypocrites that whined about the danger of having attention drawn to matters that might bruise public sensibilities and tarnish the general mind. The language that was used by those filthy Pecksniffs, read in the lurid light of recent developments, fills us with what I dare call a holy loathing beyond the power of all words to express or even suggest.

Now that is our city government, and what is this town going to do with it? Is there a man in New York, provided only he even imagines himself to be respectable, that with the case boldly put to his conscience, dares stand up and tell even his own heart that he is going to vote on the side of municipal dishonor and governmental rot? A hundred years from to-day history on this side, and on the other side of the Atlantic, will be in some measure what the momentous issues of this week make it. The country is witnessing us. The nations from afar have diligent eyes fixed upon us; the years to come are going to frame their purposes from the material of this week's verdict.

May the mighty Spirit of God so possess this vast metropolis on the coming Tuesday, as to lift us momentarily out of the tainted atmosphere we are breathing, draw us into visible fellowship with those overarching realities that abide through all the days and years, reveal to us the pregnant possibilities of the supreme moment, and cause the enlightened and earnest citizenship of New York so to mass itself upon the one grim and muscle-knotted foe that we have to meet, that from this time on virtue shall mean more, vice be painted blacker, despair seize the beggarly mob that have been trying to filch the jewels from our municipal crown, and the door be opened to a nobler future of American dignity, prosperity, and power.

## CHAPTER XXIII

### VICTORY—ITS PERILS AND OPPORTUNITIES

Two months have elapsed since election, and we are now in a situation to understand with considerable clearness, both how much and how little our victory denotes. There has been elected to the Mayoralty a man with a clean record, and one who did not purchase his election by mortgaging his administration either to any party or to any individual aspirants. He entered upon the discharge of his duties untrammelled; he was elected on the platform of non-partisanship, and our confidence in the honest obstinacy of the man is so entire that we believe he will devote himself unswervingly to the work of actualizing the non-partisan principle.

Mayor Strong is going to put into the positions of administrative and executive power, men whom the city will respect. It is almost paralyzing to reflect that in the course of six months, if Albany does not prove an obstructionist, the administrative boards of the city will be filled with men whom we shall be glad to honor; men whom we should not be ashamed to recognize or to admit to the intimacies of our circle of acquaintance.

"Excise Board," "Police Board," and the rest are expressions that have so long awakened in our minds feelings of aversion and of contempt, that it is only by a mental strain we can conceive of a situation wherein these same terms will be suggestive to us of decency, gentlemanliness, and intelligence. That is one of the results which we can anticipate with assurance. Mayor Strong will have to be a different man from what he is to-day, and pass under the control of influences that he would to-day indignantly spurn, before he will knowingly allow any man, whom he believes to be knavish and depraved, permanently to occupy in the city any official position of trust and power. That is a great tribute to render, and it is a great expectation to cherish. It will differentiate the coming three years from the past three as widely as man is differentiated from the voracious beast which Tammany has delighted to accept as the symbol of its own brutal spirit and purpose.

Besides the results which have been wrought within our own city, there needs to be mentioned, also, the impulse which has been given to municipal reform throughout the country. There is scarcely a town of any considerable size, North, South, East, or West, that is not considering the same problems as those which are engrossing us. The movement was, to a large degree, caught from New York, and the defeat of Tammany Hall in November carried with it an impulse making for the overthrow of any number of little, unorganized, and unchristened Tammanys the country through. All of this we are authorized to rejoice in and to be grateful over. And it is not because we prize accomplished results so lightly, but rather because we estimate them so highly, that we desire to see them a continuous possession, and are impelled, before bringing our volume to a close, to consider certain elements in the case that menace our present situation, and that threaten to dissipate the glorious success consummated on the 6th of November.

Our municipal victory never could have been gained except as the outcome of popular enthusiasm. Now, while there is a power in enthusiasm, there is also a peril in it; nothing will coagulate so quickly as blood, and nothing chill so readily as enthusiasm. The moral temperature of this town marks several degrees under what it was two months ago. We do not mean that the town is less moral than it was then, but that its moral appreciations are less tense. The aroused indignation of the city was what gained the victory, but its indignation would not reach the same fever-point at seeing itself despoiled of the fruits of victory. It takes a good deal of integrity to become righteously indignant; but it takes a vast deal more of integrity to be able to keep righteous indignation in stock—to be drawn on at sight.

This city is jealous of its rights, but not yet sufficiently alive to its rights to have its jealousy a permanency. One reason of that is that it has been so long since the will of the people has counted for anything here in New York, that we have most of us gotten a little out of the habit of thinking that it ought to count for anything. This is one of the lessons that we shall have to learn. We have been for a good many years municipally enslaved, and it is going to take time to reacquire the art of being sensitive to interference with our civic rights. We are a population of a million and a half, and yet two years ago the question of the Mayoralty was decided by one man. The rest of us had no more voice in the matter than we had in the choice of the President of France or of the Pope of Rome, and yet we went on singing with traditional complacency our old hymn, which sounds well in church, but means nothing on the street:

> "My country, 'tis of thee,
> Sweet Land of Liberty."

Now, while it has been necessary that the popular conscience should be quickened in order to our becoming relieved from the immoral despotism under which we have suffered, there is a good deal more work that will have to be done before we shall be in situation to break ourselves loose from all despotism, moral as well as immoral. If we have gotten rid of the devil, or at least some of his angels, the next thing to get rid of will be the dictators which, however decent superficially, are likely to be first-cousins of those angels; and this second emancipation is a matter of greater difficulty than the first, and will require more time and effort and training. It is an amazing fact, that much as we talk about liberty, and noisily and fervently as we celebrate the Fourth of July, the number of people, even of the intelligent classes, that decline to be "managed," is comparatively small; and if citizens who are above forty-five are so rusted into the habit of being "bossed," then the bulk of our effort must be put into the work of preventing men who are under forty-five from ever getting rusted into that habit.

If I were to mention the greatest lesson which I have learned during the past three years, it would be that of the damnable dangerousness of a professional politician, and it is a truth that needs to be sanctified to the devout consideration of the citizens of this city, that we have not gotten rid of that in getting rid of Tammany Hall. As to the rank and file of people, they are right, and we can afford to trust them. The nearer we come to them and the more deeply and sympathetically we enter into their experiences and circumstances, the greater the confidence which we feel warranted in having in them. The people must be trusted. When the issue presented to them, as in the recent campaign, is a distinct one, they will appreciate it and seize upon it.

Now, the professional politician is the people's natural enemy. He takes a professional satisfaction in manipulating the people's interest without having any moral appreciation of the significance for good or evil which those interests involve. He is like a man playing at chess, who enjoys handling his pieces without those pieces being representative to him of any other value than what attaches to them as gaming implements. It is not intended to say that every man who officially concerns himself with these matters is animated by the spirit we have just specified; sweeping vituperation would be unwarranted and in excessively bad taste. Still the professional politician, understood in the sense above indicated, is a popular enemy; his watchword is diplomacy rather than principle; he is made dizzy by travelling a straight line; he values a situation according to the number and variety of combinations into which it admits of being developed, and has no interest in municipal reform for the reason that it constricts the area of his versatility.

In the earlier part of our three years' struggle, we came into no contact with politicians. The promise of success was so small as to engender in their breasts no temptation. It was only when it began to look as though something might come of it that they commenced to survey the movement with telescopic composure, to figure on the chances of issue, to rouge their bloodless complexions with a thin wash of affected enthusiasm, and to lubricate their disused machinery with reference to possible contingencies. We first struck the track of this species of ravening wolves early in 1894, about the time when Albany began to act on the matter of sending down an Investigating Committee. There was a good deal of quiet demonstration along the same line after the Committee had been designated and had held its first "reception" at the Metropole. A large amount of elaborate activity of the same sort was expended in shaping the Committee's preliminary work on election cases, which were emphasized primarily in the interest of partisan capital, not with an eye single to the weal of New York City. It asserted itself in the matter of counsel to the Committee in the bringing of W. A. Sutherland into the scene, and in the consideration of some other names that never became a matter of public record, and that were considered only with a view to their political availability.

Once the investigation got well under way, it moved at the push of its own momentum. When Mr. Goff had dived down and brought to the surface one or two specimens of salient corruption, the aroused popular feeling would brook no interruption of the work, and the politicians had no show. Politicians are like bats that fly around only when there is nothing else in particular going on. There was too much going on between May and November to make either their wings or their beaks of much service. Still, even during that time, the work of the investigation had a certain amount of shape given it by the fact of an approaching election. I believe that the Committee, and certain influences that were at work upon them, had their regard concentrated on election, and not on the particular weal of the city. The hardest blow was put in, and the consummating disclosure was arranged to be histrionically exhibited on the Saturday night before election. We are not to be understood as criticising the dramatic conduct of the investigation, except in view of what transpired later. At election, things stopped; and when they were resumed, the investigation was no more like what it had previously been than a parade is like a battle-field; and when it finally adjourned, instead of concluding in a climax, as was the case just before election, it stopped with a slump. We are censuring no one; we are simply stating what everybody in this city understands, that there were influences playing in and out of the investigation that were not operating with an eye single to ends for which the Committee ostensibly came down here, and for which they were asked to come down. This does not undo the splendid work which they accomplished, but illustrates the fact that politics has no genius for directness and thoroughness, and that a politician is not quite happy so long as he is doing precisely the thing that he seems to be doing—being in that respect like a man who is cross-eyed, who goes one way, but looks two ways while he is about it.

At the date at which these paragraphs are written (January 17th), the Investigating Committee's Bill has not yet been reported at Albany; but we venture the prediction that the form in which it will appear will bear out our previous statement, and that a good deal more of it will be dictated by political scheme than by municipal exigency. New York City wants thorough work done—a policy in which a politician has no interest or confidence. He never tucks in the ends, for he wants ends left hanging to which to tie the threads of his own chicanery.

All of this reference is solely for the purpose of illustrating the ground upon which our next battle will have to be fought. We have won a splendid victory, but it is no part of the purpose of the politicians, the dictators, and the "bosses" that we should be allowed to make that victory completely available. Political bosses are fond of miscellaneousness, as rats like rubbish, for it gives them something to nest in.

It is this obstacle that Mayor Strong is likely to confront. The citizens of New York insist that he shall be independent. The politicians insist that he shall be bitted and bridled, and it is conceivable at this date, that although the city demands that he should have the power to remove the heads of departments, that power will not be conceded unless he comes to an understanding with Albany and Tioga as to who will be put in the places of those who are removed. It would be vastly better for the city to be under the government of Tammany hold-overs, than to be under the direction of men, however decent, that are put into position at the expense of the Mayor's surrender of a part of his proper authority, and of his sacrifice of a measure of his self-respect and of our respect for him. It would, in the long run, be better for the cause of good municipal government, that the Tammany members of our city boards should serve their full term, than that better men should be put in their stead at the expense of the Mayor's capitulating with self-constituted dictators who consider the city's necessities only as so much material for aggrandizing their power, and handle the interests of a great municipality with all the bloodless unregard with which a billiard-player drives his balls or chalks his cue.

One of the most serious considerations suggested by the situation is, that the work which has been done by the Society for the Prevention of Crime, the City Vigilance League, the Good Government Clubs, and the Committee of Seventy, can hardly be considered compensating work, if it is only to issue in three years of oasis in the midst of a continuous desert of corrupt city government. If we had failed on the 6th of November, it would have been exceedingly difficult to arouse this city to a renewal of its endeavor two years hence; but if, now that we have won, the *victory itself* proves a failure, and if, at the end of Mayor Strong's term, we are left with zeal abated and ranks divided, it will be an even more difficult task to rally the city to a renewal of the struggle and a repetition of the triumph. It is time for us to be considering the bearing which each administrative act is going to have on the question of the continuance of honest administration after the present mayoralty term has expired.

More than 100,000 men voted in November the Tammany ticket. We won by a margin of less than 50,000 ; so that the shifting of 25,000, made up of the dissatisfied and the disappointed who voted for Mr. Strong this year, would easily carry the victory back into the camp of Tammany—and Tammany never dies. There will always be a Tammany in New York City, whatever may be the name or no-name by which it may be distinguished.

That which secured for us the victory in November was the power of the appeal that was so variously and repetitiously made in behalf of a clean, straight city government, administered in the interests of the city on purely business principles. That watchword gained us the victory, and it is only by adhering to that watchword that we shall retain the victory through the years and years to come. It is the supreme ambition of our Mayor to be loyal to the principle of it, and any man or clique of men, any boss or junto, that works divisively and so relaxes the bonds of coalition which gave us the victory, and which alone will be competent to give us the victory again, is a traitor to the city and to all its vast and complicated interests, and is worthy only of municipal outlawry and hot civic damnation. It was a serious question whether we should win in November. It is now a far more serious question whether we are going to make that victory the foundation of a permanent victory, and whether there are men and women enough among us who are sufficiently devoted to this city, sufficiently fond of righteousness and appreciative of civic liberty to hold themselves steadily and compactly in line, prepared to crush every movement that threatens to operate disruptively, and to bid defiance to every self-constituted despotism that dares to convert men into playthings, and to fill its veins with the warm blood which it sucks from the municipal life. Eternal vigilance is the price of liberty. It is harder to use success than to win it. Municipal ground will always have to be a battle-field; and may the God of battles multiply his champions, solidify their ranks, put might into their arms, chivalry into their hearts, and crown us all with a steady and widening victory.

www.ingramcontent.com/pod-product-compliance
Lightning Source LLC
Chambersburg PA
CBHW021955220426

43663CB00007B/825